There Came A
Lion

Carole H. Camak

Jesus sets you free!
Matthew 11: 28-30
Carole H. Camak

WinePress Publishing
MUKILTEO, WA 98275

There Came a Lion
Copyright © 1997 by Carole Camak

Published by:
WinePress Publishing
PO Box 1406
Mukilteo, WA 98275

Cover by Jon Denham

Printed in the United States of America

ISBN 1-57921-056-2
Library of Congress Catalog Card Number: 97-61741

Dedicated to James Xavier Camak V
My Best Friend

I know a man so free—

    so sure of his own worth,
    that he accepts it with neither pride nor humility.

He's so sure of who he is
    and the value of his work,
    that his wife is free to explore the horizons of her life.

He's not afraid she may reach some mountaintop without
    him, or love him less as her interests grow.

He puts up with dinners that are sometimes late.
The house isn't as tidy as it was before—
    but she laughs more
    and has more to say at the end of the day
    when he comes home to a woman
                 Who has opened a door
                 Unseen before—
    who wants him to look with her
                         and wonder....

    I know a man so free—
    And best of all,
    He loves me.

Acknowledgments

I thank my God every time I remember you. He has given me special people, like you, to encourage me, lift me up, walk hand in hand through the journey, and believe in this lifetime project. It is such a joy to call you my friend. You are a constant reminder of God's love.

Special Thanks:
To all you dear people who have faithfully attended HIGHER GROUND Bible classes looking for the lessons in the trials. You have enabled me to make myself vulnerable for the cause of Christ. Seeing the victory we share in Christ and watching Him weave His lessons in your lives has shown me the need of telling this story.

To Jack and Lonnie Carter. God moved you to Georgia to introduce me and many others to the fruitful ministry of Christian Women's Club. The time I spent as the receptionist in your orthodontic office helped me relate with confidence to others in need. Thanks for adding certainty to my journey.

To all the ladies at Christian Women's Clubs. Each time you heard my testimony and asked, "Do you have a book that tells the rest of the story?" you unknowingly motivated my drive.

To Florence Littauer, president of CLASServices, Inc. I had a book inside; you provided the tools to make it tangible. Only eternity will reveal the true dividends on your investment.

To Dale Hokrein. A fine young journalist who willingly shared the call of my heart. Through editing and editing and editing, you helped me weave the rough drafts of my journals into a story that paints a picture of God's deliverance and provision.

To Anne Coxwell and Mary Dant. Two dear sisters in Christ who see yourselves as novices when I see you as seasoned professionals. Your time and counsel were priceless. You didn't know what you were getting yourselves into, did you?

To Dorothy Barrow Atwell. While daily dealing with your "lion of physical disability" you have been my encourager, my inspiration and my "mom" by choice. Thank you for your steadfast faith and love.

To my family. Our four sons and one daughter, who impacted my life with joy, challenges and unconditional love. Thank you for believing in me and Jesus. Thank you for blessing our family with your life-partners and all those precious grandchildren.

To Eleanor Phillips Hammond. The one I lovingly called "Mama" who walked the path of fear and rejection with me and then joined in to walk in Truth. Although she is in heaven now, she insisted that I share any detail of her life to help others experience the forgiveness she knew and the freedom she came to treasure. Whenever I remember Mama—I do so with great joy.

Finally, I am forever grateful to the lover of my soul—*Jesus Christ*— who set me free! Forever!

Contents

ଉଆଉ

INTRODUCTION

A s a child I felt that people fell into two main catego-
ries—readers and nonreaders. Having a strong drive to always be actively involved, I never enjoyed reading a book. The
required book reports in high school were dreaded assignments
that I put off until the night before they were due. I assumed
that people who liked to read were lazy and lived in a fantasy
instead of the real world. Nonreaders, on the other hand, were
the ones you could count on to get things done.

Recently I had the joy of viewing the movie *Shadowlands*,
the life story of author and scholar C. S. Lewis. In one memorable scene, Mr. Lewis, played by Anthony Hopkins, asked one
of his students why he read so many books.

"I read books," he said, "to know that I am not alone."

That answer encouraged me to continue writing this book.

It was not until after I accepted Jesus Christ in September of
1969 that I changed my view about readers and literature. A
friend had given me a book titled *Through Gates of Splendor,* and
on a very cold January day in 1970, with my three sons away in
school and my two-year-old daughter taking her long morning
nap, I was deliciously alone, so I decided to read.

By the time I finished the book that day, my life had changed.
I read about the life and death of five missionaries deep in the
jungles of Ecuador, and I wept uncontrollably. Their pre-emi-
nent desire had been to carry the gospel to people who had never
heard the good news, and I could not understand why they died
what I considered to be such an untimely death. As I fervently
and sincerely asked God for some explanation, I experienced a

brokenness I had never known. Grief and hopelessness flooded my entire body. I picked up the book again, hoping to discover that the story I had just read was not true at all, because I longed for things to work out the way I wanted—with happy endings.

Then I turned the page. The author wrote as if she heard my thoughts: "In case you are thinking, 'Why, God? Why would you allow this to happen,' please read on."

In the remaining pages I found a detailed listing of many of the direct results that had come from the life and death of these five men.

Many young men had surrendered to become missionaries; others continued the work the martyrs had begun; and missionaries, already on the field, were encouraged to remain faithful. Eventually, contact was made with an isolated group of people called the Auca Indians, and the gospel message was heard and received. Perhaps the greatest message to me came through the widows of the slain men who chose to stay in Ecuador. They didn't talk of revenge or fear—instead they talked about a desire to work with the very men who had murdered their husbands. This was not the final chapter but was, in fact, a beginning for me.

This book moved me to a deep commitment. In tears, I surrendered my life to God afresh.

"God," I prayed, "the faith of these men and women made a difference. I am willing to live in total abandonment to you."

I felt God speaking to my heart. Like turning the final pages in the book, I became aware of God's desire to reveal His plan for my life. I felt no fear but felt instead a sense of awe and anticipation, which convinced me that these moments were just the beginning.

In the quietness of my soul, I heard God saying, "If you will allow me to make changes in your life, your life can make a difference too. Keep a record of what I am going to do, and one day you will write it in a book so others will know how to slay the giants that come in their lives."

I knew nothing of the giants that would come. I certainly did not see myself as a writer. But one thing I did know, God had spoken to my heart and had given me peace I had never known before—and I was willing to do whatever He desired. Immediately, I picked up a legal pad and began to write the details of that encounter with God. Over the years I have kept a journal of events that have occurred in our life as a family. My heart was made sensitive to God's work as He changed me and set me free from the bondage that I was unaware that I was living in. Today, I know what it means to be free indeed.

That day the story of David and Goliath came to mind. When David volunteered to fight Goliath, he had confidence in God and not in his own ability. King Saul offered the shepherd boy his own royal armor, but David refused. Without donning heavy armor, he had been victorious in facing the lions and bears that had come to harm his father's sheep. He would stand against Goliath in the same way. Right then I knew I could be victorious in slaying my future giants if I trusted God in dealing with the lions of life.

In this book I'm giving you a glimpse at some of the lions that have prowled into our family's life. Some of them have been ferocious, hungry for our destruction. Others, I believe, were for our instruction—to keep us alert to the lion tamer's call. We now know the same God who delivered David, and we also know He can deliver us. We, too, have faced lions and giants with confidence, victorious only through Jesus Christ our Lord.

Today you may fear circumstances of giant proportions. Maybe you're crippled by an imaginary giant. It can appear in human form with superhuman size and strength. Giants produce a state of bondage, either voluntary or involuntary. Just as the Israelite spies in Numbers 13:33 viewed themselves as grasshoppers when compared to their imaginary giants, how you perceive your giants can mean the difference between victory and defeat.

Jesus came to set us free from the bondage of this life. Only when we are free can we make a real difference in our world. As we trust God for deliverance from the lions of life, we can surely trust Him for deliverance from our own personal giants. He will not fail us. If, as you read this book, you identify with any of the same lions in your life, please know I've written about them to help you know you are not alone.

It has been said, "Strangers are friends we have never met." I don't know what caused you to pick up this book and read this far. Maybe it was the cover or the title or maybe a friend's recommendation. Whatever the reason, I say *Welcome Friend!* This is our time to visit together, and we won't be strangers anymore. Let's go forth to be giant slayers!

CHAPTER 1

⊙◊◊◊◊◊

LIONS, TIGERS, AND BEARS, OH MY!

One warm spring day I hurried to the high school to see Leda, our only daughter, who was participating in her first track meet. I knew very little about track. For many seasons Jimmy and I had watched our three sons play football, but today would be a new experience for me. Leda seemed to be a natural for the track team. Her height and long legs enabled her to feel comfortable with cross-country runs, and for months she and her best friend trained together, running every afternoon.

I rushed to make it on time but arrived a few minutes late. The meet had already begun, and I was angry with myself. Finding a seat on the bleachers where I had a clear view of the oval track, I focused in on the competitors. Leda was way out front. The rest of the girls were running together in a group behind her. I was so proud. I felt like the mother of a successful athlete.

After several laps around the course, however, I noticed something strange. The rest of the girls reached a certain point and stopped running. I couldn't understand why all of the other team members decided to stop at once. Then I realized Leda had not been leading the pack, as I had thought. She was still running. She had been trailing the other girls instead of leading. After what seemed liked a long time, she came to that same point on the track where the other competitors had finished, and she stopped running too.

Later, while driving home, finally Leda said, "Mama, what did you think of the track meet?"

"I liked it," I said, trying to be careful not to give myself away. "I am very proud of you."

Then I knew that I needed to be totally truthful and tell about my first impressions. Leda and her friend burst into laughter.

"Mama," Leda chuckled, "you should know from all those years of watching my brothers play football that we Camaks are not the fastest runners, but we do hang in until the finish."

She was right. I did not understand the purpose of a track meet. While a runner might have a good beginning pace, nothing counted until she finished the course. Since this was Leda's first season on the track team, her speed did not equal that of her teammates, but at least she hadn't given up. Leda had remained in the race until the finish, so her participation could be counted for her team.

That day at the track meet, I learned that it helps to understand the game plan. Together Leda and I built a memory that even today produces a smile when we share it. I always remind her that it did not matter that she was not the best runner. I was very proud of her willingness to participate at all cost.

Later, I recalled the track meet and its surrounding events. What a learning experience that was. I realized how much it reminded me of life. Many participants have big showy beginnings, but somewhere along the journey of life, they drop out and fail to complete the appointed course. Perhaps they look back instead of keeping their eyes on the finish line. It is easy to play the blame game when things don't go according to our plans. We can even go through most of our life whining over our difficult beginning, forgetting that the very things we call handicaps are often designed to make us strong. A bad beginning can be a lion that constantly prowls through our memory, preying on our fears of defeat.

There are many accounts of successful winners who refused to quit. Open any history book and you'll find great leaders who overcame difficult, if not disastrous, beginnings to go on to live exemplary lives, catching the attention of those who followed. If we allow rejection to discourage us, we may never know the thrill of victory.

Today, when I hear someone complaining about the hardness of their beginnings—tough childhood experiences—I cannot help thinking of my own husband's difficult start. No doubt he is the one from whom Leda received her spirit of tenacity.

Jimmy was born in 1932, and as a seventh-month delivery, he started life with some serious handicaps. He weighed a mere three pounds. His early start was complicated by the absence of a fully developed palate in his tiny mouth. This rough start enabled him to rise above his circumstances again and again, and from these formative days, he learned early that the race is never over until you cross the finish line. Life was tough.

Jimmy and I grew up in the same church family. Many times our youth group would schedule talent shows to raise funds for youth activities, and everyone knew that Jimmy was a sure bet as a contestant. He played a banjo and could pantomime Spike Jones records. He never showed nervousness or stage fright, and since he was the best talent we had, our entire show often centered around him.

Although he had a speech impediment, he lacked nothing in confidence. One day he shared with me his secret. As a child he had been required by the school system to take speech classes to improve his speaking ability. It was hard at first, he acknowledged, but later, as a teenager, he felt that the hours of practice were paying off. In order to help overcome his shyness and fear of rejection, his mother made him go into public places to pay her utility bills. He learned to speak with others out of necessity.

He was given no choice. What started out as a handicap became a source of inner growth and development.

As we anticipated the arrival of our own first baby, I became concerned about Jimmy's difficult beginning. I hardly noticed his speech impediment, yet I wondered if it was the result of his premature birth or a hereditary defect. Should I be concerned about our own baby being born with a cleft palate? All these questions needed to be answered for my own peace of mind.

Since I did not feel comfortable enough to approach Jimmy's mother with my concerns about his birth, I decided to talk to his Aunt Claire. Aunt Claire and Uncle Herbert Hair lived in a house that was on one side of Granddaddy Hair's house, while Jimmy's family lived in the house on the other side. Such proximity meant there were few secrets in their family. I knew if anybody could answer my questions, Aunt Claire could.

Jimmy often talked about the unconditional love that Aunt Claire had shown to him, helping him learn to read and often offering a home to Jimmy when his own home life was so stressful. I had come to the right person, and I was not disappointed. She lovingly answered my questions and assured me that Jimmy's birth defects were not hereditary, but instead were a result of his premature birth.

At the time of his birth, the doctors did not expect Jimmy to survive, Aunt Claire said. Unlike the modern neonatal nurseries of today, no special provisions were available for the care of a premature infant with a severe handicap. Attending physicians told Jimmy's parents that it would be best for them not to get attached emotionally to their new baby, since he would not live.

Aunt Claire continued to fill me in. She told me that Jimmy was kept in a hospital nursery away from his mother; but three days after his birth, Jimmy's mother asked his father to go to the nursery, sneak their son out, and bring him to her room. She told her husband she just wanted to see her son one time, but when he returned to her room, Jimmy's mother was dressed to go home.

"I have him now," she said, clutching the tiny bundle in her arms, "and I'm taking him home with me."

Nurses hurried around in a state of panic. Doctors followed the determined couple to the elevator, trying to convince the mother to give up her baby. She would not heed their pleading.

"Go ahead and take him home," one doctor said in desperation. "He won't live through the night."

I wondered how the doctors could have been so cruel. I'm sure they felt it was the best advice, but it seemed so heartless to me. The very thought of being denied access to my own baby overwhelmed me with a mother's compassion. Just then, I was glad that Jimmy's mother had been so persistent, but I wondered if I would ever be able to be that strong.

Although Jimmy's mother, Opal, never openly shared her feelings with me, I now felt a new level of admiration for her. She was a beautifully striking woman. Her dark stylish hair was peppered with premature gray. Though she appeared very aloof, I felt that one day our relationship would grow into a genuine love and acceptance of each other. Unlike my own mother, who was overly involved in every activity at church, Jimmy's mother did not attend church regularly. Although she possessed many creative gifts and talents, she chose to live a very isolated life. To my knowledge she did not open up to anyone.

Aunt Claire told me that life with a premature infant—outside the hospital—was very confusing for the whole family, especially in the 1930s. She helped all she could with the daily care, but she certainly did not know how to handle an infant with a severe handicap. Jimmy's mother was frightened in her new responsibility.

Once they were home, Jimmy's father asked an old family doctor to make a house call. He came immediately to check this tiny bundle of life, and after examining Jimmy, he wrapped him in cotton for protection, then told them to do the best they could. Having no incubator, the next best thing seemed to be to turn the small nursery into one. Even though September days in Georgia are warm, Jimmy's parents placed a small heater in the room to raise the room temperature and draped a blanket over the small bassinet to keep drafts away from the newborn. So began the tedious process of caring for such a fragile gift.

As Aunt Claire described those early days of Jimmy's life, I thought about all the books I had been reading in anticipation of our new baby—the pros and cons of breast feeding, the importance of bonding between mother and child. I realized that feeding must have been very difficult for an infant with a cleft palate, and I was right. Aunt Claire told me swallowing was difficult for Jimmy. Breast milk was secured from his mother and dropped carefully from an eye dropper into his tiny mouth. Many times he would strangle and choke on the milk.

From hour to hour, it looked like all their efforts might fail. But slowly Jimmy began to adjust, and within his first months he began to gain a little weight. Experimental surgery was performed to try to reconstruct the missing palate. It would be essential to his very survival.

What a traumatic beginning. Everyone had hoped that the additional responsibility of their handicapped child would restrict Jimmy's parents' party life and rebellious attitudes. It did not seem to affect them one way or the other.

Now my fears were eased about my own baby's birth, and I asked Aunt Claire to tell me everything she could remember about Jimmy's early life. Knowing that Jimmy's father had died under suspicious circumstances left me with pieces of the puzzle that did not seem to fit. I loved my new husband and was beginning to understand that many of our adult attitudes are influenced by our past. I felt a need to know everything about his early life so I could understand him better. Jimmy had told me that his mother would never talk, even to him, about what had happened to his father.

Once again Aunt Claire came to my rescue. It was so obvious to me that she loved Jimmy as if he were her own son. Tears flowed down her cheeks as she talked of the suffering and hardships he had endured.

In June of 1933 James Camak, Jimmy's father, graduated from the University of Georgia School of Law, at the age of twenty-one. Ten months after his son's birth, while on a visit to his father's home in Athens, Georgia, James and his young wife attended a party. Sometime around midnight, after returning home from the party, an argument began and a shot rang through the quiet house. Jimmy's father lay wounded from a gun shot to his head.

Questioned by her father-in-law and the Athens police, Opal could give no satisfactory answers. Who pulled the trigger? Was it an accidental shooting? Only she knew the details. After three days in the Athens hospital, Jimmy's young father died. At the request of Mr. Camak, Jimmy's grandfather, the police dropped the investigation. With such a life of promise cut short, what would happen to the family now?

Jimmy's father had been an only child, since his own mother had died just months after giving birth. The elderly grandfather and his bachelor brother, Uncle Louie, were left alone in the large family home in Athens. Aunt Claire told me that on several occasions, Mr. Camak asked Opal to move to Athens so Jimmy could grow up in the familiar surroundings his own father had known. She refused.

There was no evidence of joy or happiness in the Camak home in Athens. Visits were limited due to the strained emotional circumstances. His only grandson now lived miles away in Augusta, Georgia, with his mother and her family. Grandfather Camak decided the least he could do was to make sure all of Jimmy's financial needs were met.

Now Opal had a mind of her own. Raised as the only daughter of a very strict father, she had chosen to live a lifestyle that was considered different by her family and one that others thought was just plain wild. As a teenager she would sneak copies of *Modern Romance* and *True Story* magazines into her father's house. My own mother had heard about the repeated searches by her family that often ended in confrontations between father and daughter. This may sound a bit mild when compared to the pressures we live with today, but every act of rebellion has a beginning step.

On a few rare occasions, Opal reminisced about the better times in her early months of marriage to James. As the only female in the family, she had been the center of attention and said her father-in-law had catered to her every whim. The large Camak house, which sat in the middle of a city block in Athens, was a beautiful three-story brick home with all the appropriate furnishings. Had she chosen to live in Athens after her husband's death, her life would have been well above her own lifestyle in Augusta.

After one year on her own, Jimmy's mother remarried. Aunt Claire said she hoped this marriage would bring a sense of stability to Opal. It was not to be. The new husband, Broadus Bequest, made his living as a pool hustler, and family life became more stressful. Eventually, he became a motorcycle policeman working the night shift, and what little life the family had together was arranged around the stepfather's schedule. The weekends were filled with parties, drunkenness, and arguments.

Through the years Jimmy has shared with me about the many times that, as a preschooler, he lay in his bed listening to his mother and stepfather arguing in the next room. As the arguments intensified, Jimmy once heard his mother shout to her irate husband, "Give me your gun. I'll just settle this argument here and now." Back and forth they would threaten each other.

"Go ahead and shoot if you want to," he said. "I don't care what you do."

Alone and afraid, Jimmy knew there was no place of escape. Their small three-room house had very thin walls, and Jimmy heard every detail of the arguments. Many times the fighting lasted well into the morning hours. A little boy, with fear in his heart, lay helpless night after night, hoping he would not hear a gunshot.

We may think we have outgrown our memories, but then a scene from a movie or some present-day event will trigger remembrances of our past.

For instance, I have always enjoyed watching true-life stories in movies or on television. Jimmy, on the other hand, always left the room to find something else to do. For a long time I could not understand why he was not interested. One day Jimmy told me.

"Carole, I don't want to watch that kind of real life story," he said. "It brings back too many painful memories. I don't have to hear about child abuse or domestic violence in order to identify with it—I lived it!"

Then I understood his deep hurt. Years later Jimmy was able to find recovery and healing, and today he doesn't run when he hears true life events. He has found the answer to his pain.

Over a Christmas holiday we had the opportunity to walk through a wonderful museum of trains and toys from years gone by. As we walked through the exhibit hall, we could overhear comments from other people. Once we heard someone from our generation or older say, "Oh look, son. I had a toy car just like that one when I was your age."

"Oh really," the child said unenthusiastically, then dashed off to see the next exhibit.

This child did not share his parent's excitement over the toy. The adult stood there, gazing at the toy that had opened up a storehouse of memories, and before long he engaged another museum visitor into a conversation. It was as if the parent wanted someone to talk to and to share the memories with. He needed someone who cared enough to listen.

Not all memories are pleasant. Recently, while viewing the movie *Forrest Gump*, I realized that Jimmy was experiencing a painful flood of memories, and they were overshadowing his enjoyment of the story. "Jimmy," I whispered, taking his hand, "enjoy the movie, don't relive it."

A special squeeze of tenderness told me he would try. I knew the movie dredged up painful memories for him. I had heard him tell of the disappointments of his own childhood. As a small child with handicaps, life in Jimmy's neighborhood had been full of exposure to the pain of misunderstandings. Even now it was tough remembering.

At the age of six, he dreamed of making friends at school. First grade can be traumatic for anyone, and Jimmy's first days were no different. Excitement turned to fear. One day the teacher asked each student to stand and read aloud. Jimmy panicked. He tried desperately to locate his line in advance. When he stood up to read, his mind froze. His fear of speaking had produced a mental block. After struggling through his line, the children laughed.

"Why do you talk like that?" they would ask, holding their nose in order to mock his speech.

He didn't know why he talked differently. After he tried to explain, they only teased him more. All he wanted from his classmates was acceptance. His dream turned into a nightmare. For the first time he became aware of just how different he was from the other children. The mocking of the children, coupled with his fear of failure, gave him a glimpse of just how cruel his world would be.

Each afternoon when school was over, Jimmy said he would walk home alone. The wooded area surrounding his neighborhood became his escape, and the world of childish fantasy helped take his mind off of the cruel things happening in school.

One of the few bright spots in his young life was his extended family. In the afternoons Aunt Claire would patiently work with Jimmy to help him learn to read. Over and over they practiced—*See Dick run. Run, Spot, run!* On weekends Jimmy's Uncle Herbert and his Grandfather Hair would give him old boards and nails to construct little projects in their yard. That time was not wasted. Even today Jimmy can fix almost anything around our house. But his extended family's daily influence was limited. Jimmy's mother and stepfather were very angry, resenting anyone in the family who they thought was trying to interfere.

Jimmy spent two years in the first grade. Then two years in the second grade. The neighborhood children were moving on up to the fourth and fifth grades, but Jimmy was always left behind to greet the new class. He hated being the oldest in the class. The new children always asked the same question, "Why didn't you pass your grade?" It was especially painful because he did not have an answer.

One day during Jimmy's second year in the third grade, his teacher asked him to stay after school. Quite often he had been kept in after school hours for misbehaving. This time was different. The teacher wasn't upset; instead, she showed compassion. She began to tell him a story about a young man named David and a giant named Goliath.

She described David as a young boy, perhaps about Jimmy's size. Jimmy wondered about the giant. He had never seen anyone nine feet tall. "Why, the giant's head must be huge," he thought. "What kind of shoes did he wear? His shadow alone would be frightening to someone the size of David."

Jimmy identified with David in his choice of weapons; after all, the teacher said David used a slingshot to kill Goliath. The excitement of that afternoon's story made him feel so free. He wondered what he would do if he were to see a giant like Goliath.

The walk home that afternoon was another beginning for Jimmy. For the very first time, he realized that his life was full of giants. There was the giant of speech. The giants in his home life. The horrible giant of being different from the other children. His entire world took on "giant" proportions. But now he knew of a boy named David. The teacher had told him that this story came from the Bible and that God loved him just as He had loved David. It was the encouragement he needed.

That night he prayed for the first time in his young life.

"God, this world is my giant. If you could help David slay a nine-foot giant, I know you can help me."

Although Jimmy did not fully understand the process, in simple childlike faith, he believed. All he knew to do was to ask God to make tomorrow better than today, and it became so. He began to see a purpose in his life, and instead of dwelling on his troublesome home life and difficult beginnings, he now felt loved and accepted. Remembering the story of David helped Jimmy face each day's giant with courage. Through the Bible story, God became real and personal to him.

After six years of education, Jimmy was promoted to the fourth grade. Now he would attend another school. With a new sense of confidence, Jimmy could hardly wait to go. One giant down. This new school was a four-story grammar school located in the mill section of town. At last he would leave his reputation behind and start over. The best part about his new school was that he was not so different there. There were many boys as old as he was in his same grade. Because they had repeated several grades, it was not uncommon for some of the boys to get married as soon as they finished the seventh grade.

It was a new beginning, but he soon learned that life had not really changed. The boys would come up to him, hold their nose and try to talk the way he did.

One day early in the school year, a bully and several other boys gathered around. They were looking for trouble.

"Why do you want to fight me?" Jimmy asked. "I just want to be your friend."

Other boys joined the circle of onlookers. It did not matter how much he tried to reason with them, they only seemed more determined to prove a point at Jimmy's expense.

There was no way out of it. Jimmy prayed silently.

"God, here I am, just like David. David didn't start his fight, and I didn't start this one. But God, you helped David slay Goliath, and I am counting on you now."

During this and the many fights to follow, he waited for the first blow. Then he would hit with every ounce of strength he had. Of the six fights he found himself in during those first few weeks of school, he didn't lose a single one. He defeated boys who were a head taller and much heavier than he was. Soon everyone around the school knew better than to start a fight with Jimmy Camak. Though he was smaller, he had something extra going for him. It was another beginning.

God's faithfulness to Jimmy gave him new confidence; for the first time, he knew he was not alone. His grades improved and so did his outlook on life. He now felt a responsibility to God. He wanted to be the best that he could be.

Many times I have seen Jimmy reach back into his own storehouse of experiences to help our children, as well as their friends. He always reminds troubled teens that they are not alone. Remembering the power he gained from the story of David the giant slayer, Jimmy shares the story again and again.

At the age of nineteen, he felt confident to find his own way through life. Soon he would be choosing a career for himself, and along with his friends, he decided to join the armed services. The military rejected him. Not one to be discouraged, his next move was to prepare himself with an education, and electronics seemed to be the fastest growing field. Television was just coming into its own. In order to pursue this field, it would be necessary for Jimmy to move to another city. He did not mind making a move—it would be a welcome opportunity. Even at this time, his home life was stressful. His mother and stepfather offered no emotional support at all.

Jimmy decided to enroll in a television technical school in Chicago, Illinois. He had never lived away from home—new giant on the scene. To travel above the Mason-Dixon line would open up his world, but what would the people be like? Would they accept a Southern boy from east central Georgia? On the way to Chicago, Jimmy prayed and asked God to lead him and help him make the right decisions. Once again he felt like David.

While this giant was new and as yet unknown, Jimmy felt confident that God would be faithful to lead the way. Victory over one giant did not mean he was home free. Somewhere lurking in the shadows of the unknown were the other enemies waiting for their time to spring into action.

This reminds me of a time when we had out-of-town guests. After a short trip around our community, we turned from the highway and started up our long, winding driveway, past tall hardwood trees scattered among Georgia pines. A blanket of fallen pinestraw and leaves covered the ground. Their two-year-old son began to whisper in hushed tones.

"Lions, tigers, and bears, oh my! Lions, tigers, and bears, oh my!" he said, crouching down behind the front seat.

The view from the car window helped my little friend create in his mind the scene of anticipation from *The Wizard of Oz*. Today, remembering this experience, I think of how many times we face life with the same outlook. On any given day I could probably say, "Lions, tigers, and bears, oh my!" Life seems to be a jungle full of threatening encounters. We all have them. So how do we recognize and handle them?

Isn't it interesting how we face change with uneasiness? Feeling a bit insecure about living up north, Jimmy wanted to maintain his contacts with the same denominational church with which he was familiar. Arriving at the school, he requested help in locating a place to room. Several leads came from the housing file, and he went off to check them out.

The very first address he found happened to be the home of Mrs. Thompson. She rented two rooms to four boys and had one vacancy left. He took it. He was the youngest one. The other fellows had recently been discharged from military service and were going to school under the GI Bill. The age difference didn't seem to be a problem, and soon they all became buddies. Life was better than ever.

Through Mrs. Thompson, Jimmy discovered that in Chicago, a city 35 miles wide at that time, there were only two churches of his preferred denomination. Fortunately, Mrs. Thompson belonged to one of them. Again, this was the encouragement he needed. He had prayed and God was leading. For three-and-one-half years, Chicago was his home. Mrs. Thompson loved "her boys" as she called them, and her loving care filled the void Jimmy had felt in his own home. She darned their clothes and gave them true mother's love. Lasting friendships developed with several of the roommates and eventually with their families. Forty-four years later we still correspond with several of these fellows.

Many years have passed since that teacher told a story to a little boy who desperately needed a beginning. Since then, Jimmy has fought in countless battles. His faith has deepened. For fifteen years he served as an elected member of our county school system. At the beginning of each school year the board members are allowed a few minutes to address all the employees of the school system. Jimmy never missed the opportunity to share his early experiences of school life with those who deal with children every day. Today he is a respected community leader.

Several years ago our son Jody was a patient on the pediatric floor of our local hospital. Jimmy shared the details of his own difficult birth with our pediatrician. Within the hour Jody's doctor returned to our room with an unusual request.

"Jimmy, will you come with me to visit someone in another room?" he asked. "A young mother who has just admitted her infant son to this hospital needs to hear your story."

Continuing with his explanation, the physician told us that two months earlier the woman's son had been born with a cleft palate like Jimmy's. The mother was too frightened to care for her son. Feeding time was especially difficult. She would try to nurse the baby, but the possibility of strangling him on the milk frightened her. It was robbing her of the joy of even holding him close. The time was right to begin corrective surgery, but she was not sure she could allow the procedure.

"Of course," Jimmy said. "I will be happy to do anything to help ease her tension."

Once the initial introductions were over, the pediatrician slipped out of the room. Jimmy began to share some of the struggles of his early months of life. As he talked about the difficult feedings and the eye dropper, the frightened mother began to relax. Here was a grown man who had survived a difficult beginning in the primitive medical year of 1932.

Finally, she agreed to the corrective surgery. Her baby came through the surgery with flying colors. The technology was so much improved. Before we left the hospital the next day, we both visited that room. Mother and baby were doing well.

Years later, as Jimmy shared his testimony at one of the county-wide school board meetings, a young teacher, tears in her eyes, approached him.

"Mr. Camak," she said, "you probably don't remember me. I'm the mother you talked to in the hospital six years ago."

What a reunion. The timing for their meeting in the hospital had been just right and had resulted in a new beginning for a mother and her son. While she had Jimmy's attention, she proudly showed pictures of her healthy son. He was like any other well-adjusted six-year-old.

"Thank you for caring," she said tearfully. "I will forever be grateful that our paths crossed and that you shared your story with me."

Remember, it doesn't matter how you begin. The important thing is that you stay in the race to the finish. Just when we think a piece of clay has been marred, God can fashion a beautiful and useful vessel out of the broken pieces. Don't let one bad beginning define the remainder of your life. Identify the lions and the giants and learn to deal with each one appropriately.

Let's Consider the Lion of Bad Beginnings

Each new day is a fresh page in your book of life. It does not matter where you have been; today is a brand new opportunity to be all that you can be. The past is out of your control, and the future isn't even here yet. So you have this moment right now to make a decision.

Ask yourself, "Am I willing to take a step into the unknown, or will I cling to the past with its giant hurts, mistakes, and disappointments?"

Recently, a sight-impaired runner in the Paralympics was asked to explain what kept him motivated to compete.

He said, "I cannot see my competition, I have never seen the finish line, but I have never lost my focus on the goal. I am in the race to win."

The choice is mine and yours. We can keep our eye on the goal and stay in the race, or we can drop out because of difficulty. One thing is for sure: We cannot move forward while always focusing on what is behind. It would be like attempting to drive a car forward by looking in the rearview mirror. Disaster surely awaits, progress will be limited and the journey boring.

Often the door to freedom is locked tightly with the key called "forgetting." The memory of a bad beginning haunts the opportunity to begin again. Once, while sharing with a friend about forgetting what is behind, I challenged her to do just that.

"How can I forget what happened?" she asked angrily. "It would take shock therapy treatment to erase my memory of that painful event."

Realizing the controlling power of her memories, I had to agree that forgetting would present a real test of commitment on her part. Then I remembered a walk we had taken together just months before. While in the midst of her lovely flower garden, a bee suddenly stung my friend's face. The sting caused her face to swell almost immediately. Even though we treated it with medication, her face became red and the pain persisted for several days. I asked her if she remembered that sting.

"The pain was terrible," she said.

"Does it still hurt?" I asked.

At first her reaction to such a ridiculous question was obvious. "Of course, it doesn't hurt *now*," she said.

The simple illustration had drawn a word picture. She had to admit that while she could remember the bee sting, the resulting pain and swelling were gone. A confident smile replaced her frown. When we release our memories of pain to God, we may still remember the event, but the sting is gone. It is possible to forget what is behind and press on toward the goal, as we read in Philippians 3:13–14.

Perhaps you realize that you are unable to keep up in the race of life because you are encumbered with excess baggage. It could be a painful childhood experience that produces fear in your heart even today. Perhaps the deliberate deception of a trusted friend or leader has made you reluctant to trust again. Circumstances that were unfair and out of your control should never be allowed to burden you with false guilt. Do not be discouraged. Make a decision now to release anything that has the potential for holding you back. God has called you for a purpose, and you dare not try to pursue the goal while pulling a wagonload of guilt, frustration, and blame. First, surrender your baggage and then enter the race to reach the goal. Don't let a bad beginning define the rest of your life. You can be a winner if you keep pressing on.

See you at the finish line!

Chapter 2

ᏩᎳᎤᏉ

Known By the Lion Tamer

When in doubt, read the directions. That statement sounds easy enough, but I find it hard to do. My husband teases me about only reading directions when all else fails. He's right. For some reason directions confuse me. When a sales promotional describes a product as "user friendly" (meaning, of course, that if you follow the step-by-step plan there should be no problem), I have to chuckle to myself. Obviously, they haven't taken my temperament into consideration.

On our first trip to California, we became acquainted with those wonderful information clerks strategically located in tourist areas. After listening to our inquiry, the clerk would take a magic marker and begin to draw a line on a printed map. With the map positioned on the counter facing us, it was easy to understand the directions that followed.

The knowledgeable clerk would point to a place on the map and begin by saying, "You are here!"

How easy life would be if we could have someone say, "You are here! Follow these markers and you won't go astray."

This was certainly not the case in my younger days. With no well-marked path to follow, it was easy to blame someone or something for each dilemma. To acknowledge my current position would be to admit responsibility. Instead, around every bend and turn in the road, the lion of placing blame crouched ready to give me an easy excuse to defend my insecurities and failures.

Just as we have to have a starting point for life, we also have to identify our present location in order to proceed to our desired destination. Perhaps, for many of us, we become aware of our position in life from comments we hear regarding our birth order. This is one event that is totally out of our control.

"I was the middle child," I like to tell my family, "long before it was known that the middle child is supposed to be the problem child."

Consider firstborn children and you'll understand what I mean when I say birth order is one of the primary indications of our expectations. Do you know a firstborn child who has not struggled with perfection? Always trying to live up to expectations can be very stressful for any family. Then, of course, there is the only child. Without the benefit of sibling rivalry, how can he or she ever understand sharing? Worse yet, to be the baby of the family often leaves the impression that you are spoiled beyond belief. While birth order is blamed for many ills of society, we cannot change it. A word to the wise: You are where you are in the family and nothing can change it. Accept it and go on.

I heard a story about a lady who stopped to ask for directions to a certain exit on a superhighway. She was told that she had about a hundred fifty miles to go. In disbelief she said, "How can that be?"

The reply came back, "Well, it's a hundred fifty miles if you keep going in this same direction. But, if you will turn around, you will reach your destination just ten miles down the road."

Isn't that the hardest decision to make? To turn around and go in the opposite direction requires a willingness to listen and make necessary changes. It is always helpful to ask directions from someone who knows the right way, but just because someone dispenses directions with a confident manner does not mean that they know what they are talking about. I have often found myself on a wild goose chase when given unclear or false information. All too often I've been led astray by someone who did not want to say, "I don't know, you had better ask someone else."

False information can be costly and cause dangerous misconceptions. Take children, for example. Early in life they are taught to trust and obey without asking questions, and because of inexperience and desire to please, they can easily be given incorrect information by those who are in authority over them. This places a large responsibility upon adults to take seriously their role as advisors.

Recently a program on television demonstrated the ease with which a stranger could gain the confidence of children. While several small children played on the playground, their parents were interviewed by an adult conducting an experiment. Without exception, the parents claimed their children would *never* follow a stranger out of the park. But when a gentle-speaking grandfather figure approached carrying a picture of a small puppy he claimed had strayed away, each child agreed to help this stranger find his pet. One of the parents, who had been sitting on a bench just out of hearing range of the child, was shocked. His child had disregarded specific instructions not to talk to strangers and had responded without thinking of the consequences. Obviously, the children responded more to the persuasive nature of the present stranger than to the instruction of the absent parent.

Most of my childhood memories are centered around our church life. Attending church was a delight. Since our mother and our grandmother went to every meeting, my sisters and I had no choice. We were regulars at every Ladies Aid Society, missionary meeting, and Sunday school class function.

Funerals were no exception. Many times while attending a funeral, I would consume a considerable stack of tissues, wiping the steady flow of tears. It was easy for me to cry. Identifying with the bereaved, I would place myself in their shoes and feel their grief. Mama never cried, and often after a funeral, she would scold me for crying. As a way of teasing her, I often referred to my mother as "Hardhearted Hannah," thinking that her lack of tears meant she did not care. I could not understand why she was so cold until many years later when I learned that my mother did indeed care, but her coldness was her defense against becoming emotionally vulnerable.

Our church was a place where my mother, Eleanor Hammond, visited with her friends and found a place to belong. She made it a second home for me, and I remember the nights I fell asleep in the service. The benches were hard with no padding, and in the summer, the constant drone of the ceiling fans lulled me toward dreamland. Shortly after the pastor began his sermon, I would whisper the same question in my mother's ear.

"Mama, may I lay my head in your lap?"

Always the answer was the same.

"No, just rest your head on the back of the pew; service will be over soon." She knew that if I fell asleep with my head in her lap, I would drool on her starched dress.

I soon learned a method to get my way. I would whisper to my mother that I felt sick and thought I may vomit. For some reason she had a fear of one of her children getting sick in church. Perhaps she feared the embarrassment. In order to avoid that possibility, she would tell me to go outside alone, and that is exactly what I wanted to do.

The car seat was softer than the church pew, and I slept until she was ready to go home—not when the service was over, but much later. My mother and her friends always stood in front of the church talking until the one light that illuminated the church entrance went out. I am grateful that we didn't have the dusk-to-dawn security lights that are so popular today. I guess she would have stood there talking all night.

Church is also the place where I had my first encounter with an information clerk who gave faulty directions. I was nine years old and my Sunday school teacher was someone in my life who, because of her position, easily influenced me. She shared information that led me to make important choices, choices that held eternal consequences. One year she chose Easter to teach about life and death. Putting her regular lesson aside, she began by telling us that when we died, we would either go to heaven or to hell. For several minutes she described how glorious heaven would be—no sickness or pain or suffering there. The streets were paved with gold and the gates were made of pearls. From her glowing description I pictured heaven as a magnificently beautiful place.

Before the class was over, the teacher also painted a vivid word picture of the horrors of hell. She told of the darkness and the intense flames, of how there were no flowers or gentle breezes there. I wondered how she could describe both places so well if she had never been to either of them. My imagination began to run wild.

Suddenly, the spell was broken when a boy in the class asked a question we all wanted to ask.

"How can I know that I will go to heaven when I die?"

"Oh, that is easy," she said waving her hand in the air as if to dismiss such a question. "You need to become a Christian."

That sounded all right, but then he asked the most pressing question. "How can I become a Christian?"

Again she gestured with her hand, "Oh, that is easy too. You need to join the church. Then you will be a Christian, and you will surely go to heaven when you die."

In her explanation about heaven and hell, my Sunday school teacher never once spoke of assurance of salvation. In fact she never used the word *saved*. In a statement that was sure to keep us all on our toes, she explained that we would have to live a good life and do good works. She said that we would not know our eternal destination until after death had occurred, and on Judgment Day when our good works were measured against our bad works, hopefully, the good would outweigh the bad. "What a labor for the rest of my life," I thought.

All afternoon I thought about nothing but heaven and hell. That evening my mother and I went to church together. The time seemed right. With all of my pent-up emotions, I announced my desire to join the church that night. This brought an unexpected response from my mother.

"Why tonight?" she asked.

"I don't want to go to hell when I die," I said quickly. The information gained from my Sunday school teacher that very day prompted my spirit of urgency.

My mother tried to convince me that I was not going to die anytime soon, but it did not change my mind. All the way to church my mother told me she did not think I understood what it meant to be a Christian, and we argued back and forth. Motivated by my fear, I was more persuasive.

We never talked about the doctrine I was supposed to understand. I know today that my mother did not understand it either. Finally, somewhere between home and church she gave up.

"Well, okay, if you are sure you understand, you can join tonight," she said.

That evening I sat with my friend just a few rows from the front. I told her about my decision to join the church. She was already a member and was very happy for me. I don't remember a single point that was made in the sermon that night, but when the service ended and we stood up to sing the invitational hymn, I felt a sudden sense of fear. The aisle seemed to be three miles long. How could I walk down there alone?

Turning to my friend I said, "Peggy, what do I do now?"

Without pausing for a minute, she gave me the helpful information I needed. "Go down about halfway through the second verse. That's when most people join."

So, halfway through the second verse of "Almost Persuaded," I walked down the aisle. The pastor at the front had known me from birth. He took my hand, looked me straight in the eye and said, "Carole, do you believe that Jesus is the Son of God, and do you accept Him as your personal Savior?"

Well, of course! I thought everyone knew that Jesus was the Son of God. I didn't know what a personal Savior was, but being familiar with the customary answer, I said, "I do."

"I know you do," he said tenderly as he placed a loving arm around my shoulder.

What a relief. Having my name on our church roll would enable me to participate in the baptismal service the following week. Somewhere I had heard that even when you joined the church it was not valid unless you were baptized in water. The baptismal pool was only filled when needed. That meant it would be next Sunday evening before I could be baptized. Based on that information, I was fearful that even if I did join that night, I would have to live carefully for the entire next week so as not to upset God.

By Wednesday evening prayer meeting, the church clerk presented me with my own set of offering envelopes. There was no doubt now. If they wanted my offering, I must be a valid church member. I felt more comfortable about my future. The joy of following the instructions of my Sunday school teacher gave me a certain sense of acceptance for which I had secretly longed. Even though I had been given the wrong information and was moving in the wrong direction, it would be years before my path would be challenged by truth. I was excited about being a church member. In my heart I felt I had checked off the necessary requirements and needed to make no additional changes in my lifestyle.

Gradually life became complicated. There were only two official churches in the area where I attended public school. All of my friends attended either Grace Methodist or North Augusta Baptist. If, like my family, you belonged to any other church, my classmates considered you to be a heathen. I found myself trying to explain to my classmates at school why I was a member of a different kind of church. I did not understand the differences, but I argued relentlessly. What had started out to be the answer to my fearful dilemma became the source of painful words from friends. No one had given me any information regarding the obvious misunderstandings I would encounter from friends.

A popular rhyme was believed to take the sting out of harsh words: "Sticks and stones may break my bones, but words can never hurt me." It's not a true statement. Words do hurt. Sometimes through a person's weakness, words can become almost a self-fulfilling prophesy. For example, being told, "You will never amount to anything," can actually place an imaginary ceiling above a child's ambition. Just as a computer can only release the information that has been programmed in, we, too, find that the labels assigned to us affect our attitude.

Today, I cringe when I hear an adult address a child using belittling terms. Children should be taught respect for others and healthy self-esteem. We cannot accomplish positive results when we are busy attaching labels that will hobble their progress. While we may think it cute to identify a child with their position in the family or by some attitude they have displayed, care should be taken to instill positive goals. Negative associations will reap detrimental results and they should be prohibited.

Our local newspaper often lists an obituary by the given name of the deceased and then includes a nickname in quotation marks. Nicknames can become so well known that lifelong friends may not even know the proper name of their friend. I have seen such a variety of nicknames. I cannot help wondering just where they began. Was it a result of some experience, or perhaps an attitude?

One day my husband and I were attending a county fair, and he directed my attention to an elderly gentleman across the park.

Jimmy said, "That man's name is 'Hunkie.'"

"You have got to be kidding," I said. "What kind of parents would name their son Hunkie?"

Then I heard the rest of the story. When this man was a little boy, he and a friend stole a Good Humor ice cream cart. They ate all the ice cream bars that were labeled *Hunkie*, and from that day on he earned the nickname "Hunkie." To this day, Jimmy cannot tell me the man's real name.

Environment plays an important part in a person's life. Without specific information, we learn how to act by observing the values and responses of a parent. This was made clear to me several years ago when our family was visiting with an elderly couple that lived about forty miles away from our home. As we started to leave, Lael, our six-year-old, put his little arms around our dear friend and gave her a little pat on her shoulder.

"Cousin Bessie, if you need us for anything, just give us a call."

With a smile on her face and tears in her eyes, she looked up at me. "Carole, he learned that from watching you."

Cousin Bessie knew as well as I did that a six-year-old could do nothing tangible to help her. Her blessing came from knowing that Lael had observed tenderness and love. As young as he was, he was already reaching out to those in need.

For children, peer pressure, coupled with the desire to belong, often breeds incorrect information. It certainly did for me. Because my family chose to attend a different church, I was unable to participate in the weekend activities of the local churches. Every Monday morning my school friends talked excitedly about the fun they had experienced, and I felt excluded. No matter how hard I tried to fit in, I was an outsider.

Eventually, my life turned in a new direction. With the decision by E. I. Dupont to build a large facility in our area, our little community seemed to explode. Until this time, there were only enough children to fill one class per grade at our public school. In no time the school added four classes per grade to take care of the influx of new students. With this increase in population came all manner of church denominations: Presbyterians, Catholics, Lutherans, Episcopalians, and nondenominational groups. At last I was not alone. Others belonged to "unofficial" churches, and no one gave them a difficult time about it. Finally, I felt accepted by my peers. I guess there were just more of us to argue with. I found that I could fade into the crowd.

It's painful to admit, but some things are out of our control. Our birth order in our family, circumstances in our early childhood development, and erroneous information we receive along the way can become stepping stones or stumbling blocks. It is up to us. Either we can play a "blame game" and blame others for our current predicaments, or we can learn from our experiences. We should be willing to ask for directions, but in the end, realize our own responsibility to pursue truth.

Am I angry about the misconceptions formed in my early years? No! There is no resentment. Although the incorrect information robbed me of years of peace, I understand now that all those who were giving me instructions did so in their own ignorance. This does not excuse ignorance. Individually we each have an obligation to know the truth before we send someone off on a wild goose chase. It is easy to assume we have all the right answers to give and not have a personal understanding of the question. When I joined the church, I knew the correct answer was "I do." The pastor who took my hand at the front of the church knew I gave the correct answer. But, by accepting my correct answer without discussing the question with me, he only confirmed the false information in my experience.

Sometimes, people who are asked for directions will try to look knowledgeable by giving an answer, whether it's right or wrong. A prepackaged answer often comes before the question is fully understood. For these reasons, when I am in need of direction, I seek someone who not only says that they know the correct information but also proves it by his or her lifestyle and experience.

Although each person is responsible for his own choices, we really do need each other. When we share an idea, ask for advice, or even offer advice based on experience, we can help one another in making wise choices. For instance, several years ago my husband was active in an investment club. The individual members would find a particular stock, research the pertinent background and present the findings to the entire group. With careful deliberation, choices were then made based on the accumulated data. Experience and successful investments proved this to be a wise procedure. There is safety in the counsel of others, provided the others with whom you consult understand the circumstance in question.

This does not mean that you must always have a majority of opinions to make a wise choice. Jimmy and I have made choices that proved beneficial, based solely on our individual research. The key is research. We, of necessity, must be scholars of truth, for only the truth can set us free from peer pressure and that strong desire to have the approval of others.

On one occasion Jimmy was presented with an option to purchase a large tract of property. He considered the undeveloped wooded area with a large lake to be a very good investment for the future. The price was right. After seeking additional financial advice from his banker, he was advised to forget the intended purchase. According to the bank advisor, this purchase was not advantageous.

With a sincere desire to gain advice and also show respect for his elders, Jimmy then asked his stepfather, Broadus, for his advice. His answer was explicit and peppered with four-letter, abusive words. Though Jimmy felt the investment to be very sound, he acted on the advice he had received from his elders and did not make the purchase.

Two years later that same piece of property was purchased by one investor for the same price for which it had been offered to Jimmy. After being divided into three large tracts, that undeveloped wooded area became the location for three major industrial plants. If Jimmy had followed through with his initial plan to purchase the property, we would have become financially secure on that one purchase.

Perhaps you also can identify with a personal loss as a result of making wrong choices. We learn valuable lessons from past mistakes. Although experience is a wonderful teacher, we should seek advice from those who are acquainted with the facts and have full understanding of the opportunity in question.

Remember, we don't have to be perfect to be loved. Once while helping a friend prepare lunch for our children, I asked her for a knife to trim the crust from the bread. She seemed very reluctant to allow me to open the cabinet drawers.

Finally she said, "Will you continue to be my friend when you find bread crumbs in my silverware drawer?"

Sensing her genuine embarrassment, I replied, "Don't be silly. Doesn't everyone have crumbs in their silverware drawer?"

She realized how frivolous her concern was and we both had a good laugh. I thought of how we allow even a close friend limited entrance into our lives. We reserve certain areas to ourselves out of fear that a friend might not like us if they know us too well.

What a comfort to know that God knows all about us and still loves us more than any earthly friend possibly could. Absolutely nothing is hidden from Him. He understands our thoughts. Before we speak, He knows the spirit of our words. He also knows when our thoughts and motives are impure. Yet, He loves us unconditionally.

A visit to the circus can prove the power needed to exercise control. While the lion tamer never turns his back to the lions, he remains in complete and confident control at all times. When I think of the lions that have entered my life, I rejoice that I am known by the greatest lion tamer of all—God. He knows the lions by name, remains in control, and carefully allows them to enter into my life.

David, the shepherd boy, faced the giant with confidence because he had identified and dealt with previous lions. I, too, have been able to deal with many lions in my life. I know that God works in this way to prepare me to handle the giants. That is still His workable plan today.

Let's Consider the Lion of Blame

Where exactly did I go wrong? Where was God when I was being given false information? If God knows all about me, why did He allow that horrible experience in my life? These and other questions consume the thoughts of many today. We have a choice. The choice is to either live crippled by false information or to live victoriously by responsibly accepting who and where we are.

In reading Psalm 139, I am comforted to know that God knew me before I was even born. He has set boundaries in my life. The most important truth to know is that He wants me to know Him. This can only come when I stop blaming others, learn responsibility, and accept that God is all-knowing and all-powerful. I am not here by accident but by His design.

Whenever I share my story of acceptance, I am made aware that all too many in my audience have gone a long time without hearing anyone say, "I love you." A life of blame and defeat has robbed them of feeling loved or accepted. Often there are lonely widows, frustrated wives, and rejected teenagers longing to be loved.

While I am speaking I pause, smile, and in my most compassionate tone of voice say, "God loves You! You are special because you are a Designer Original!"

Then, as if the years of brutal comparisons, emotional put-downs, and devastating experiences were washed away, an expression of wonder graces previously defeated faces. With enough practice we can brush off criticism and coldness, but what can we do with love?

Right now, you have a choice, either to go through the remainder of life playing the blame game or to stop and say: *I am here! I will not let the bad information rob me of joy. I refuse to live as an emotional cripple held together by negative labels applied by others. I will accept my birth order, which I cannot change, and open wide the door of acceptance to God's wonderful plan for my life. I am a Designer Original—uniquely different and designed by God. I now choose to live like one.*

Acceptance begins in the individual's heart. If I am constantly belittling myself, how can I expect others to accept me? But when I understand that God knows all about me and still loves me, I am encouraged. I can risk loving others because I am loved.

How do you see yourself? When you look into a mirror, do you concentrate on your weaknesses? Are you afraid that someone whose opinion you value would not accept you if they knew you better? When you consider some of your past painful experiences, do you blame God? Since life is 10 percent of what happens to me and 90 percent my attitude, it is easy to understand that my response is vital to my well being. Everything has the potential of making me better or bitter. I determine the result.

Learn from your experiences. If they can be changed, change them. If nothing can alter the circumstances, accept them and make the best of each difficulty. I have discovered that the very experience that produces pain in my life can become the platform that enables me to reach out to help others.

You are Here! Believe that God loves you and make the choice to live today. Acceptance will soon come! You are a designer original, known and loved by God!

CHAPTER 3

⊙⥾⥾⥾⊙

FOR BETTER OR WORSE

My father, Joe Hammond, made his living as an auto-motive mechanic at a large soft-drink bottling company. He worked long hours and was often called out in the late night hours to rescue a driver with a disabled delivery truck. Each year he was allowed only one week for vacation, which he used to participate in a fishing trip with some of his friends from work.

Family vacations were never a part of our life. One day a year Daddy would take our family to Tybee Beach in Savannah, Georgia. Leaving home hours before daylight, we would arrive at the beach at about nine-thirty in the morning. After the long ride, we were hot and eager to get into the water. During the hottest part of the day, we played in the ocean and enjoyed a picnic on the beach. Suntan lotion was expensive, so we did not buy any. Mama did not like the sun and would sit under the shade of a pier that stretched out into the water. She begged us to stay out of the sun, but we did not want to. This was our one day at the beach, and we hoped to get a great tan while we en-joyed the waves and the seashore.

Believe me when I say that we enjoyed that day, but we *en-dured* the following week. After arriving home late that night, we would fall into bed looking very much like lobsters. By morning we were totally miserable with painful sunburns and large water blisters on our shoulders. The remainder of that week, we would wear as little clothing as possible and hoped we would survive the painful burn. The next year we would repeat the same scenario.

The first year after Jimmy and I were married, he began talking about taking a vacation. I had never been on a vacation before. I was delighted at the idea of staying in a motel for a week, viewing tourist attractions, and having fun. It would be a new experience for me.

Since then there have been many wonderful vacations for our family. Several years ago, while vacationing at a rented beach house, we were reminded of the importance of having a plan for each day's activities. We began our first morning of vacation with a sigh of relief. At last all the preparation was over and we had arrived safely. Now the fun could begin.

Priscilla, our three-year-old granddaughter, appeared at the breakfast table dressed in her new swimsuit, flip flops, and sun hat. There was no doubt about what was on her mind. But, first things first. With eleven people under one roof, I naturally assumed the role of self-appointed organizer. As we sat down to breakfast, I asked what I thought to be a very important question.

"What is on the agenda for today?" Surely we needed a plan if the day was to be productive, I reasoned.

"The beach! I am ready to go to the beach *now*," said Priscilla with great enthusiasm.

We all laughed. It had never occurred to us that she knew what agenda meant. But one thing she did know: The only plan she was interested in was going to the beach.

Plans are important. A businessman without a plan accomplishes very little. Somehow time slips away and we often cannot give an account for how it was used. To be productive, we must formulate a plan. Also, it is advisable to stop now and then to re-evaluate our goals and accomplishments.

Have you ever listened to a small child share his or her dreams or goals? As the child grows, the goals change. One day a little boy wants to be a fireman, then an astronaut, then maybe a sports announcer. Goals have a way of taking on new importance as we become interested in other things. Some goals are innate. They motivate our choices from early childhood. Of course, there are people who find themselves in their thirties before they know which goal they truly want to pursue, and perhaps that explains why so many find fulfillment in later life in a different career than the one they originally were trained to follow.

Life can be compared to an ascending escalator. From the first step we cannot yet see the next level. Our initial plan is to move along, observe the view along the route, and eventually reach the top. Often we make our own plans, ask God to bless them, and then proceed full speed ahead. That might be our method, but I have observed that unless God is *first* in my plans, they become frustrating, lack spiritual purpose, and cannot succeed.

The first time that I can recall expressing my own plans and goals, I was a sophomore in high school. One day while sitting around the table in home-economics class, our teacher asked each girl to share her goals for the future. The replies varied from a career in nursing or modeling to possibly teaching school. Each one sounded more glamorous than the preceding one.

When my turn came I said, "I have only one goal. I want to meet a good-looking, Christian man. We will get married and have either four or six children. Just like the fairy tale, we will live happily ever after."

My goal seemed so clear—like a romantic walk on a flower-strewn path—I saw no obstacles to impede my intended happiness. Unknown to me at the time, a lion was lurking in my future—the lion of interference springing from my own family.

My classroom reply brought a burst of laughter and shock from the other girls.

They all said, "Is that all you want? Don't you want more out of life than that?"

I was embarrassed, but not discouraged. My teacher, Mrs. Baxley, had been a true role model. Without being aware of it, she had lovingly nourished my goal. Every day she spoke of the joys to be found in being a devoted wife and mother. Her husband was our principal, and she worked out of necessity. It was obvious that her first love was her home. I was confident that my goal, like hers, would satisfy all my needs.

Little did I know how close I was to the beginning of my goal. There was a young man named Jimmy Camak at my church. I watched him closely for several months. Since he was six years older than I, he was in the youth group with my older sister. He had returned from Chicago after graduating from the American Institute of Technology. My older sister had married that summer and moved away to another state, and I was left without a buddy. I missed her. For the first time, I felt alone.

Several life-changing events began to unfold. People do play the funniest games. My mother and Jimmy's grandmother were friends at church, and together they were playing matchmaker.

After each service at church, my mother would say, "Carole did you talk to Jimmy Camak?"

"No, I did not even speak to him," I said, revealing my shy nature. "He did not speak to me, so why should I pay any attention to him?"

I learned later that Jimmy received the same questions when he arrived home. Grandmother Clark, his stepfather's mother, lived with them. When he would go home after a youth meeting, they would sit together and talk. She would ask, "Jimmy, why don't you ask Carole out on a date?"

Jimmy told me that his reply was, "I like her, but she is too young for me."

In order to prompt Jimmy into action, his grandmother said, "Well, I heard that Carole had a date with a young man at our church named Bill."

"Grandmother, Bill is too old for Carole; why, he is as old as I am," he said emphatically.

She only chuckled and said, "If you don't ask Carole out, somebody else will."

On Christmas Eve of 1953, the youth group at our church met to go Christmas caroling. For many years we had used a large truck filled with straw to go from house to house as a group. This year, because of bad weather, we decided to travel in cars. I made sure that my girlfriend and I climbed into the back seat of Jimmy's car. My first cousin, who was four years older than I, rode up front. It was a fun evening.

As we were leaving the last house on our list, Jimmy walked up beside me and said, "Carole, why don't you sit up front this time?"

That was just what I wanted. I had joined in the game. My cousin made sure that I sat in the middle of the front seat for the ride back to the church. (By the way, I have been in the front seat now for more than forty years.)

Upon arriving at church, Jimmy offered to take me home. That sounded like a great idea. My mother would be glad that she did not have to drive alone to pick me up. Before we arrived at my home, Jimmy asked me what I had planned for the next day, and I thought that was a strange question. The next day would be Christmas, and I knew that I would be spending it with my family, as always. He then asked me if I would like to have a date. Without even asking my mother for her permission, I said yes. My mother would not object; after all, he was in my church and that automatically made him acceptable.

Christmas Day was wonderful. We visited with a couple who were Jimmy's friends. They had just moved into their new home and were pleased to have guests for the afternoon. At first I felt a little shy and insecure. We talked and played games.

That evening Jimmy said, "This has been the best Christmas I can remember since I was a little child."

Then he asked me for another date and I agreed. From that day on I never dated anyone else, and neither did he.

With my goals firmly fixed in my mind, life became like an escalator. Going up, up higher and higher. I could not see the top, but I was certainly enjoying the trip. Life began to change for me. Every Friday and Saturday Jimmy would take me out to a restaurant and then to the movies. On Sunday we attended worship services at our church, spent the afternoon with some of his friends, and rushed back to church on Sunday evening. I felt like a princess.

Almost all of our dates were centered around church functions. By Christmas of the following year, I knew in my heart that I had found the man of my dreams. All I had desired was a good-looking, Christian man. Jimmy was certainly good looking; anyone could see that. He had dark brown, curly hair and baby blue eyes. He belonged to my church, so that automatically made him a Christian, or so I thought. What else could I want. Being older than I meant he was already established in his career. By anybody's standards it appeared that I had made a very good catch. I knew a bond of true love was developing between us. Life was almost perfect.

One evening Jimmy appeared to be very serious. Normally, I was the serious and reserved one.

Finally I said, "Jimmy, what is wrong? Have I done something to upset you?"

He turned those beautiful blue eyes toward me and said, "Nothing is wrong, Carole. I have been praying about something very important to me."

Well, he could deny it all he wanted, but I knew that if he was praying about something serious, I must have done something to upset him. After all, I thought, no one prays unless there is a major problem. I certainly did not. Now his nervousness was more apparent.

Sitting up straight in the seat he said, "Carole, I am ready to settle down. Since I was a little boy, I have always prayed and asked God to lead me in big decisions. He has never failed me yet. So I have been praying and asking God to show me whom I should marry."

Now I was the nervous one. He had gained my undivided attention. As I listened he shared his dreams and goals for the future. They were like mine. His beautiful proposal was full of all of the things I wanted to hear. He wanted to share his life with me.

Finally, he finished his explanation by saying, "Carole, I believe you are the one God has chosen for me. Will you be my wife?"

I was thrilled beyond words. Without any hesitation I said, "Yes! I would love to be your wife."

At that moment it did not matter that he had not asked my father for my hand in marriage. We both knew my parents would be thrilled. Jimmy had won their hearts and an accepted place in our family. In fact, he seemed to fit in with my family better than he did his own.

At the time I wondered why he had bothered God with such an unnecessary question. God had the whole world to run. Jimmy could have saved some time if he had just asked me to marry him without involving God in his decision. But, no matter; it was done and everything would work out fine. Our wedding would not take place until I graduated from high school. In August he gave me a beautiful diamond ring. My plans for a church wedding now filled all my waking hours.

In the forty-plus years that we have been married, life has sometimes become a bit hectic. I often remind Jimmy that he prayed for me and obviously got just what he asked for. He should have no complaints, right? I must confess that I did not pray for him before I got him, but believe me, I have done a lot of praying for him since.

Life was like a fairy tale. Nothing could burst my bubble, and I was climbing higher and higher. I still could not see the top of the escalator, but wonderful things were happening. The past year had been great. I felt secure, comfortable, and loved.

Jimmy enjoyed being with my family. Before we were married, he purchased eight acres of land from my father and began construction on a lovely brick home. I would be living with the man of my dreams less than one-half mile from my parents' home.

Today there is such wonderful premarital counseling. I marvel that so many marriages of my day have survived. I believe that many would have been more successful if there had been some instruction given. The only preparation I had for being a wife came through my home-economics class. The pastor who performed our wedding only met with us for a few minutes the night of the wedding rehearsal to discuss the order of the service.

With all of my dreams for having a large family, I envisioned a close relationship with my parents and Jimmy's parents. Since they knew each other through limited church connections, surely we would share happy holidays and family events. My first warning of family friction came one week before the wedding. Jimmy's step-grandmother had a way of speaking her mind. Confident in the fact that her matchmaking skills had been successful, she set out to fashion a mother-daughter relationship between Jimmy's mother and me.

Out of both respect and a little tinge of fear, I had been addressing Jimmy's mother as Mrs. Bequest. I wanted to call her "Mom," but I dared not take the liberty to do so without her permission.

Grandmother Clark said, "Carole, you two need to decide what you will call each other after the wedding. You will be family now, and you don't have to be so formal."

There was an uncomfortable moment of silence. Nervously, I asked my future mother-in-law what she would prefer.

"My name is Opal," she said coldly. "That will do just fine."

There was something in her attitude that let me know she did not intend to allow me any closeness.

Disguising my disappointment, I responded, "All right, if that is what you want, I will call you Opal."

Opal was so different from my own mother. She was very stylish in her manner of dress and appearance, and no one I knew felt comfortable around her. She seemed distant. I found myself wanting to be accepted, but at the same time, I felt intimidated by her presence.

I was determined not to let this little detail become a barrier. I thought surely if I just loved her that someday she would ask me to call her "Mom." I had confidence that my love for her son would soften any uneasiness she may be feeling about our marriage; I could wait. But that day never came. No matter how much I tried to show her that I loved her, the coldness remained.

Love is a complex emotion. To reach maturity it must be based in mutual trust and genuine concern for each other. Generally we respond to the love that is expressed toward us. For instance, one day several years later, I was visiting with another young mother at our church. She asked if I had a son named Jody. I told her that Jody was my middle son. She then told me how her middle girl had developed a big crush on him. They were only nine years old at the time.

When I talked with Jody that evening, I asked, "Jody, do you know a young girl in your Sunday school named Cammie?"

In typical boyish fashion he replied, "No, why do you ask?"

"Cammie thinks you are the cutest boy in the whole church," I said casually, relaying the message I had heard from her mother.

Showing no evidence of interest, Jody brushed it off as if he did not care. By the time the next Sunday rolled around, Jody had found out everything there was to know about Cammie. Suddenly, she was of great interest to my nine-year-old son. Within a few weeks, Jody and Cammie were "an item" at our church. Because our families usually sat near each other, they soon found it comfortable to sit side by side on the same church pew. This is a vivid picture of just how we respond when we find out someone cares for us.

Through the years, I have come to understand love as the greatest expression of one's inner desire to be a part of another person's life. I know today that I cannot truly love others unconditionally until I have experienced that kind of love personally.

God is love. He loved me when I was His enemy. He loved me when I couldn't help myself. He loved me even though my nature was self-centered. Having experienced His love, I am now free to love others with the same genuine love that can enable me to look beyond faults to see hidden needs.

We hear a lot about love in the entertainment world; there it's often portrayed as a selfish manipulation to get one's own way. Often what is called love is really lust. True love is not selfish. It is, instead, an expression of kindness coupled with an ability to seek only the very best for the object of our love. History is strewn with broken hearts that are missing this kind of love.

Love is an action word. Someone has said, "You can do things for someone without loving them; but you cannot love someone without doing things for them."

How often we hear a husband or wife or perhaps a parent say, "Of course, I love them. They know that. I give them everything they want," when in fact, true love is best expressed not in giving things, but in giving yourself with total abandonment.

For love to grow it must have a beginning. When I was a bride, that beginning came with a spark of love that would enable me to enjoy the best of life with my husband, not only in good times but also in bad times. On Saturday, June 30, 1956, we pledged our love before God and many witnesses. It was easy to promise to be faithful in sickness or in health. We were both feeling fine. To think of being together in richer or poorer did not even present a problem. In view of my limited understanding of finances, my married life would certainly be much richer than I had been accustomed to.

After a lovely wedding, we left for a brief honeymoon trip to Florida. Jimmy had begun working for AT&T in February and had only three days off for our honeymoon—and my first real vacation. No one advised us to make reservations. In all of the excitement, we did not anticipate Florida in the middle of the July Fourth vacation rush. Each afternoon we would rush frantically, along with other tourists, from one motel to the next in search of a vacancy. I felt like we were on the Indianapolis Speedway. We always managed to find a place to stay. Our trip could have been a disaster, had we not been so starry-eyed with each other. Jimmy kept apologizing for not making reservations, but I was so happy that it did not bother me. One day we would be able to tell our children about all the memories we were gathering.

At least we had a lovely little three-room furnished cottage to come home to. Our new house would not be completed until September, and for the next two months, we rented a perfect honeymoon cottage located in the yard of a lovely old home. Our very first home came with a freshly painted picket fence surrounding it.

When we arrived I felt like Cinderella—my prince had arrived, romance filled our hearts, and all would be heavenly. With such a storybook beginning, how could we do anything but live happily ever after.

As we approached the front door, Jimmy picked me up in his strong arms, opened the door, and carried me over the threshold. We were home. I switched on the light and nothing happened. We tried several different lights and realized there was no electricity in the cottage. We did not understand. Perhaps the power would have to be switched on at the big house; we walked up together to talk with our landlord.

Jimmy said, "Mr. Fogel, something is wrong in the cottage. We have no electricity."

With a twinkle in his eye, Mr. Fogel said, "Did you pay the deposit to have the electric power connected?"

Quickly I said, "No one told me that I needed to pay a deposit for the power."

Now Jimmy felt embarrassed. He had been attending a school out of town for three weeks prior to our wedding and had given me a check to pay the first month's rent, but he never told me to have the power connected. The landlord had assumed we knew what we were doing. He suggested that we call the power company the next morning to request service, but until then we would just have to be in the dark.

No problem. We were happy, we were in love, we could handle this little inconvenience. There was only one thing to do. We drove over to my mother's house to get the candles that had been used in our wedding. Being a very thrifty person, I knew she would have saved every one that could be used again.

More memories. It was so romantic to begin our life in our home by candlelight. We did, however, miss having an electric fan for cooling. A Georgia night in July, without a fan, is something to be remembered. Without electricity we would be unable to prepare breakfast the next morning. Jimmy asked his mother if we could come for dinner that next evening with them. This was not the way I wanted to start out, but what could we do? I remember feeling so guilty because Jimmy's mother and stepfather ridiculed both of us for not knowing about the need to pay a deposit. Of course, they had not mentioned anything to us because they did not want to interfere, or so they said. This was a preview of the attitudes we would encounter throughout our marriage.

Because of the Fourth of July holiday, the power could not be connected until late Friday evening. Our neighbors must have thought that we were a very romantic couple, with all the candles. We never told them the real story.

Finally, after the electricity was cut on, it was time to start cooking, and I realized that I did not know how to cook. As far back as I could remember, I had been a faithful helper in my mother's kitchen. But she had never taught me how to prepare meals. My limited experience included setting the table, washing dishes, and cleaning the kitchen.

I needed some big-time help. I knew Jimmy liked fried shrimp, so on my first shopping trip to purchase groceries, I bought boxes of frozen breaded shrimp, frozen French fried potatoes, lettuce, and tomatoes. That first night I prepared the meal, and Jimmy was impressed. All was well. So the next night was no different. Then I ventured out. Instead of shrimp, I bought a piece of beef. It was as tough as an old shoe. Jimmy ate and never complained. Each night we had the usual fried potatoes and salad.

After several weeks of these menus, Jimmy said, "Carole, I love shrimp, steak, and potatoes, but could we please have something else?"

I was heartbroken. That was all I knew how to prepare. Once again my prince charming comforted me.

He said, "That's all right. We will work together and learn how to cook."

Over the first hump. Breakfast was easy for me to prepare. As a Southern girl, I had only known one breakfast choice. In our home everyone ate a hearty meal of grits, eggs, meat, and toast; so every morning I prepared a breakfast for Jimmy while he dressed for work. Then I found that I had another problem. After smelling the bacon and eggs, I could not eat. Why did the smell of the food I enjoyed make me feel so nauseous?

"Don't worry, Carole," Jimmy would say, "I don't feel much like eating either." Morning by morning a perfectly good breakfast would be thrown out.

We had only one car, so every morning I would drive Jimmy to work six miles away. Three times in the first two weeks, he called me at about ten o'clock to pick him up from work.

He'd say, "I don't know why I feel so bad. Maybe it was something I ate."

We failed to notice that we had not eaten anything to make us both feel sick. Within a few blocks of his office, I would have to stop the car at the curb so Jimmy could open the door and vomit. It was so embarrassing. Then he would feel better and we would go on home.

I once heard it said that love is blind, but marriage is a real eye opener. How true. My plan had been to be a mother, but somehow I never dreamed it would come so soon. When I think of all the information available today, I marvel that we were so naive. No doubt, I was pregnant. My morning sickness continued at every meal for three months. Jimmy got over his sympathetic morning sickness after about two weeks. It was difficult to be a new bride and feel so sick, but once we knew what was happening, we were both very happy.

The first flaw in my ideal picture of family came from my own mother. I had always known that she felt uncomfortable accepting the pregnancy of anyone—planned or unplanned. Mine was totally unplanned.

Her initial comment was, "Is there anything wrong with you?" The emphasis was placed strongly on the word *wrong*.

I could sense that my mother disapproved. She blamed Jimmy for what she called our total irresponsibility. Knowing that we were happy, legally married, and able to support a family made no difference to her. When I needed her support, I found it lacking. Why was she so hostile? What could have made her so negative toward pregnancy? It would be much later in our life before the reasons for her anger would surface. For now my joy over a baby was clouded by her frequent painful comments.

Nine months after our storybook wedding, we had our first son. James Xavier Camak VI was born on March 25, 1957. Jimmy was thrilled. Our son was healthy.

When we brought our son home from the hospital, we were totally on our own. Together we made formula, cooked our meals, and tried to adjust to our new responsibility as parents. Neither my mother nor Jimmy's mother offered to help. We managed the best that we could.

Jamey, as we called him, was a good baby. When he was ten months old, Jimmy and I decided to have another baby. Once again my mother was furious. By now I was beginning to expect her anger. My joy over being a mother was greater than my fear of her responses, and so Jody Paul Camak was born on November 23, 1958. Our Thanksgiving that year was very special. Our family was growing, and my dreams were unfolding just as I had planned.

A few weeks after Jody's birth, I walked toward the nursery and overheard my mother talking to her new grandson.

Cradling the tiny infant in her arms, she said, "Jody, don't you worry; I am going to love you even if your daddy does not love you."

I could not believe what I was hearing. I walked into the room and said, "Mama, what on earth are you talking about? What makes you think Jimmy does not love Jody?"

With a determination in her voice and a serious expression on her face she said, "Well, I don't think so. Anyone can see he spends all of his time with Jamey. Obviously, he does not love Jody at all."

I was frustrated. Desperately, I tried to explain that Jimmy was spending a lot of extra time with Jamey, who was only twenty months old, so he would not feel neglected. I reminded her that Jimmy had never handled Jamey a great deal when he was an infant, but I never doubted his love for him. Jamey was a toddler now, and Jimmy knew he could take him outside. Not only did that give me a break, but Jamey loved following his daddy around the yard. Nothing I said made any difference.

Finally, the conversation came to a close as she said, "You can believe that if you want to, but I know the truth. Jody will just be our grandson, and we will love him as our own."

Her attitude was not going to change. I felt anger at her attitude but also guilt for my own feelings toward her. Hoping that time would help her see the error of her ways, I dismissed the issue from my mind. I wanted everyone to be happy so I refused to let my joy with my children be diminished by any outside influence. I could not see the wedge that my mother was beginning to drive between Jody and the rest of our family.

Jimmy was a very good father. Because he worked the afternoon shift, he spent most of his mornings working on improvements of the eight acres that surrounded our home. Building two ponds and clearing the wooded area gave him a sense of accomplishment. My mornings were filled with caring for our two sons, and I became a busy stay-at-home mom.

My mother would come down in the afternoons when Jimmy went to work. She had very strong opinions about everything Jimmy and I did. Occasionally on Jimmy's day off, we would take our two sons and spend the day together. Mama would get very angry with us for not telling her every detail of our plans.

Tensions began to rise between my husband and my mother, and I felt caught in the middle. I wanted to be free to build my life with my husband, but Mama made me feel guilty for not being her little girl. I was blinded by my dreams and plans for a family. I refused to heed any red flags of trouble ahead.

A popular comedian from television used to react to any problem by saying, "When you see trouble developing, you should just nip it in the bud."

That is very good advice. It is not necessary to be on the defensive all of the time, but we should keep our eyes wide open to avoid the danger of letting our plans and dreams become an obsession.

Bitterness and resentment begin with just a small root. From my gardening experience, I have learned that if you plant ivy, you should decide where you want it to go. The first year it sleeps, the second year it creeps, and the third year it leaps. It is possible to allow outside influences to rob us of our dreams and plans. Little by little they can cripple your happiness and cause your escalator of life to come to an abrupt halt. Then you will never know what is at the top. I was beginning to learn that if a dream is worth having, it is worth fighting for.

Let's Consider the Lion of Interference

Attempting to live as if I were the captain of my ship and the master of my fate led to frustration and failure. A very simple dream soon became a struggle to keep the peace. Under constant pressure to please everyone, I tried to be the perfect wife, mother, and daughter, and interference from those outside of my marriage threatened to destroy the very life I was so intent on building.

In Psalm 127 we read, "Unless the Lord builds the house, its builders labor in vain." Plans and goals without God are futile. All of life's work, such as building a marriage, establishing a career, and having a family, must have a solid foundation established in God's will.

The family unit was the first institution God established. It is interesting that the first problem God saw in man's life was his loneliness. Long before there were schools, hospitals, and governments, God set the family unit into motion. Like a fast train, the best family can jump track when something or someone causes interference.

A marriage, by definition, is the relationship of a husband and wife. It is a gift from God and should be a commitment between a man and a woman. In Ephesians 5:31 we find the necessary plan for a healthy marriage. A husband should leave his father and mother and should be joined unto his wife. This process of becoming one should be protected against any interference that threatens its stability. Of course, this does not mean alienation of family members. Instead, the attitude of parents, friends, and other family members should be to encourage the building of a new and stronger bond between a couple. A man and wife should be working together for a common goal—a successful family unit.

My advice to newly married couples today is the same advice I received long ago from my obstetrician. After witnessing the stress my relationship with my parents caused in my marriage, Dr. "B" reminded me that I had entered the wonderful state of matrimony by choice.

"You need to be on guard for anything or anyone that might threaten your relationship as man and wife," he said. "When your children are grown, you will find yourself left with the one you started out with. It is totally up to you. If you protect your marriage, you will grow old together. If you put others first, you will be a very lonely person in your later years."

There is a delicate balance between supporting your children in their marriage and trying to control them as an extension of your own dreams. Today, all of our children are grown and married. Jimmy and I are learning to share insights from our personal experiences, but we realize that couples need space to develop their own marriage relationship.

There came a time when I had to decide who was most important in my life: my husband, whom I loved and chose to spend my life with, or my parents, who refused to release me to build my own life. In our marriage vows, I had promised to forsake all others and cleave to my husband. This meant that, since we were joined together as one, our responsibility was to be concerned for each other's welfare.

I discovered that making our plans without God is like an escalator ride going higher and higher; you enjoy the trip for a while, but sooner or later it will come to an abrupt halt. What then? It is better to surrender your plans for God's approval and find contentment in His master design.

Marriage is like a triangle. The first side is the level, solid foundation based on God's Word. The two vertical sides represent the husband and wife. By choosing to place Jesus Christ as the head of the marriage, the husband and wife grow closer to one another as they grow closer to *Him*. It is our choice.

Where do you see your marriage? Would it be described as a marriage or misery? Are you committed to one another in sickness or in health, for richer or poorer, for better or worse? How long has it been since you said, "I love you!" and meant it with all your heart? Marriage is honorable, and it should honor God!

What about your attitude toward your children and grandchildren? Have you given them any reason to respect you? Will they remember you as a loving and firm supporter or as the perfect illustration of all the demeaning "in-law" and "grandparent" stories?

It is never too late to change. Perhaps an honest inventory is in order. In Psalm 139 David asked God to search his heart, test his actions, and reveal his thoughts. When this is the sincere request of our heart, God will point out the sin and then lead us to His better way of love, freeing us from destructive interference.

Should you recognize the lion of interference in your life, don't excuse it as nothing. Left unchecked it will produce pain, resentment, and defeat. From my experience, I've found that this particular lion is the most subtle. We excuse the actions of those around us as being "just their way of caring." We place our own values to the side while we try to please everyone else. I would urge you to address the source of the interference in love—not in an angry, condemning manner, but instead, in a search for truth.

You could begin by saying, "I may be misjudging this situation, but could you help me get to the bottom of my concern?"

Often, by just making the concern known, the lion is identified. Then, healthy dialogue can begin between both parties. Hopefully it will result in establishing guidelines for future interactions.

We may not all agree, but we must give the other parties freedom to develop their own lives. Let's be on guard to never cause interference under the guise of caring. People don't care how much you know until they know how much you care!

CHAPTER 4

ᏬᎢᎠᎯᎣ

BEWARE OF THE BLACK ROCKER

On a recent visit to Colonial Williamsburg in Virginia, our granddaughter expressed interest in the unusual signs displayed over the shop doors. Instead of clearly written words, there was a picture of the particular item to be found in the shop. We explained that in colonial times the majority of people were unable to read. They could distinguish between shops by a picture. A picture of a shoe indicated a cobbler shop, while a picture of a bonnet represented a hat shop. It made shopping easier, no doubt.

Color-coding is often used to move traffic along in a large hospital. The bright colors painted on the walls have a specific purpose. The information clerk gives directions by instructing you to follow one color until it is intercepted by another color.

I'm amused today as I recall an incident at the Atlanta airport. While waiting for the underground train, I was instructed to stand on a color-coded circle. I must have looked like a frightened child in kindergarten. That mental picture reminds me of how many years I spent standing on an imaginary color-coded spot to please my own mother. My life traveled by like a fast train. For fear of disappointing her, I obediently stood where she said stand, adopted the same values as she, and held on for dear life. My mother was becoming my idol.

Early in my marriage, I committed myself to a ride of a lifetime. Every day I tried to be a good wife and a good mother. Often I found myself feeling torn between pleasing my husband and trying to live up to my mother's expectations. I struggled to keep things peaceful at any cost. Jimmy tried to be patient with me in my immaturity. Aware of my strong loyalty to my mother, he was becoming very uncomfortable with what he perceived as conflict. A strong spirit of competition was developing. A bride and groom are usually symbolized on top of the wedding cake, but in our marriage, a strange triangle was developing—the bride, the groom, and the mother-in-law. I was caught between my desire to please my husband and my desire to please my mother. It became a very delicate balancing act.

My first face-to-face encounter with the lion of idolatry came on my first Mother's Day. Our first son was only six weeks old. Jimmy had asked his mother to babysit so he could take me out for a nice dinner in a restaurant. This was her first time as our babysitter. We had a lovely day, and Jimmy was so excited about my being a "new mother." I felt so special.

That afternoon we visited my mother, Jimmy's mother, and his two grandmothers. We were thrilled to have our families living close by. Since I had grown up with a custom of giving gifts to mothers and grandmothers, I had purchased a gift for all four of them. It was a memorable day.

The next day when Jimmy came home from work, I heard him struggling to get in our back door. When I walked into the kitchen, there was a beautiful black Boston rocking chair.

In a very stern tone of voice he said, "Happy Mother's Day!"

I was surprised, but confused. Why was he talking about Mother's Day a day late? He proceeded to explain what had happened that day. He told me that my mother had called him at work and told him that if he really loved me he would have given me a gift for my first Mother's Day. I could not believe her nerve.

She had gone on to say, "Poor Carole was so disappointed and hurt that she did not get a Mother's Day gift. I think you should buy her the rocking chair that she really wants."

This shocked Jimmy. He was not aware that I was disappointed. Thinking that he had certainly shown his love to me the day before, he had no idea that he had disappointed me. The fact that my mother had called him at work and addressed him in such a bitter tone of voice puzzled him at first, then it made him angry. As soon as his work day ended, Jimmy went to the furniture store and bought the chair my mother had so clearly described.

His anger was evident. Like a pebble dropped in a pond, the ripple effect of this Mother's Day was growing even wider. I wasn't disappointed. I had admired this chair earlier, but we already had a nice new platform rocker that I used every day. When I saw the pain and obvious hurt in Jimmy's eyes, I did not want the chair at all. He refused to return the chair, and I refused to sit in it. So it was placed in a spare unfurnished bedroom for an entire year.

Many times over the years I've told this story about the black rocking chair in hope of helping others. It is easy to see the trouble that can come from insisting on having your own way. It is far better to do without than to be the unhappy owner of a source of contention between you and someone you love. After all, we should love people and use things rather than love things and use people.

This was just the beginning. The imaginary train ride that was my marriage was taking me around the first major curves along the track of life. We tried not to talk about the black rocker but soon began to see other signs of interference in our family life. Try as hard as we could, we had no power to alter the partiality that my family chose to show toward our second son. He was totally innocent, but he benefited greatly from their favored love. When Jody turned one, my parents showered him with expensive gifts. That same year, Jamey, then almost three, received a pair of black socks. Being a child, Jamey did not realize the difference in the gifts at first. He was always appreciative. I, however, was furious. No amount of talking seemed to change my family's attitude toward our two sons. I made excuses for their behavior and even tried to compensate for the differences they showed.

The friction continued. Jimmy's mother began to favor our oldest son. For some unknown reason, both grandmothers had chosen their favorite grandchild and entered a subtle arena of competition. Jimmy and I decided to have another baby. Perhaps with three grandchildren the situation would correct itself. It is amusing how we try various options to cope, rather than dealing with the real issue.

This pregnancy was difficult. For some reason, my ride to the top was getting sidetracked. At three months, a miscarriage began to threaten. The doctor put me to bed for total rest. My older sister, who lived in another state, was also expecting a baby. Prior to knowing that I was pregnant, I had mailed all my accumulated maternity clothes to her.

One evening while Jimmy was at work, my mother came to visit me, and I mentioned to her that I would have to ask my sister to send me some of the maternity clothes. My mother got very upset with me.

"Carole," she said after a brief pause, "I don't think you should ask your sister to return anything to you. You can just go out and buy more clothes so you won't hurt your sister's feelings."

When she saw my confusion, she went on to say, "Maybe something will happen and you won't need the clothes."

I was devastated. That my mother was more concerned about my sister's feelings over some maternity clothes than the precious baby I was carrying was too painful to accept. When Jimmy came home from work about midnight, I shared my deep hurt with him. He was very kind and tried to help me understand. I did not understand. I felt confused by what appeared to me to be indifference and harshness from my own mother.

I had a very restless night. Around six o'clock I began to experience severe pain. Jimmy wanted to call our obstetrician right away, but I would not let him. Edna, the young girl we had hired to help me with the housework, would not arrive until nine o'clock. The possibility that we might have to go to the doctor's office meant I needed Edna there to take care of Jamey and Jody. I did not feel comfortable calling Mama to come down to keep them.

Jimmy placed a call to the doctor. He was already on duty at the hospital. He told Jimmy to bring me in to let him check my condition. At this point I felt so bad that I did not even realize that I had begun to miscarry. It did not occur to me that I would be admitted to the hospital. As soon as Edna arrived to care for Jamey and Jody, we left for the hospital.

Jimmy offered to call my parents, but I saw no need to call them until we knew something more about my condition. Upon our arrival at the hospital, I discovered that my doctor had already arranged for me to be admitted. He felt sure that a miscarriage had occurred and I would need to have a surgical procedure called a D&C. Suddenly and without warning my train was traveling too fast and seemed to be out of control.

Jimmy said, "I am going to call your parents to let them know what has happened."

I did not argue. I was hurting, frightened, and wanted them to know.

After the surgery I returned to my hospital room. Jimmy stayed with me all day, and we both felt very sad. Anxiously, I waited for Mama and Daddy to arrive. Finally, about seven o'clock that evening my mother and her friend from church appeared.

Her first words to me were, "Well, now you know what a D&C means."

Tears flooded my eyes. I said, "Mama, where have you been all day? I expected you to come sooner."

She made some excuse about having a lot to do at home. Intense feelings of rejection from my mother only compounded the painful loss of our baby. After a brief visit of fifteen minutes,

Mama and her friend excused themselves and said they were going shopping. In the quietness of my hospital room, once again I was puzzled at the insensitive reaction my mother had to my obvious distress. What had I done wrong?

Dr. "B" was aware of the tension I had with Mama and decided to keep me in the hospital for a few extra days. Two days later was another Mother's Day. It had been three years since I received the black rocking chair. The memories of my first Mother's Day were still painful to me. Although I loved my mother very much, she had a way of keeping emotional hurts alive.

My parents and my younger sister arrived to visit. I was glad they had come to see me. Mother's Day was a symbolic day in our family and church. It was our custom to wear a red rose if your mother was living and a white one if she was dead. Since I did not have a red rose pinned on, my sister took hers and pinned it onto my gown. We both cried.

The emotional moment was shattered when Mama spoke in a very hostile tone of voice.

"Why are you pinning that flower on Carole?" she asked. "That is a waste of a good rose."

The tears flowed freely down my face. My dear husband was at home with our two sons, and once again I was alone in a very stressful family crisis.

"Mama, why do you say things like that?" I asked.

"You don't need a red rose because you don't need a mother either," she replied bitterly.

My father was a very quiet man. He would leave the room rather than be a part of any type of discussion. He viewed every difference of opinion, no matter how small, as an argument. But this time was different. He could see the pain in my eyes and the hostility from my mother, so he finally spoke up to try to clear the air.

"Carole, perhaps your mother is hurt because Jimmy did not call us when you came to the hospital on Friday," he said.

I said, "Jimmy did call you, as soon as we arrived and found out that I would be admitted."

"Oh no," he said, "You came at six o'clock, and he did not call us until nine-thirty."

I could not convince my father that I was not admitted to the hospital at six. Why were they so confused? Where did they get the idea that I went to the hospital at six o'clock? Finally, the truth came forth. Apparently, a girl who worked at the hospital switchboard had overheard Jimmy's phone conversation with my doctor. Jimmy told the doctor that I had been in pain since six that morning. After hearing this she picked up the phone, called my parents, and told them I had been admitted to the hospital at six o'clock.

No amount of explaining helped. They believed what the girl said and refused to listen to me. Over and over I asked my father to consider the facts. First of all, Edna did not arrive at my home until nine o'clock. If I was admitted at six o'clock, who would have kept Jamey and Jody until nine? I thought common sense and reasoning would help them see that we did not leave two toddlers alone.

"I don't know," he said. "But I do know that you came at six o'clock like that girl said."

Years later when this event would come up, and it did many times, I would try to explain it again. It was always to no avail. My parents chose to believe a stranger instead of believing their own daughter. I began to learn that some people would rather believe what suits their way even when it is proven to be false.

The family is under great attack today. Perhaps the greatest enemy we face comes through the nicest family members. Often unintentional interference can divide loyalties and apply intense pressure. They erode the very strengths that God has established. The best pattern for a healthy family is the one found in Scripture. Only when we are building "one family under God" will we build better families that will stand together through the trials of life.

The only way I knew to handle my unexplainable hurt over the strain in our family was to ignore it. I tried desperately to hold on to my dreams and ignore the signs of stress. All I wanted was peace in my family. I tried desperately to cope, unaware that the stress growing between Jimmy, my mother, and me would reach greater proportions.

Sometimes we find ourselves traveling faster and faster without any control over the twists and curves of the road. Determined to keep a firm grip on our life, Jimmy threw himself into more intense work around our eight acres of land. From eight in the morning until two-thirty every afternoon, he and a young eighteen-year-old man named John worked together to build fences and clear wooded acreage. After lunch Jimmy would go to work at AT&T, and I would gather our little brood to prepare for the night.

Our house was a secured fortress. I liked the fact that we were isolated from any neighbors. When Jimmy left for work, I made sure my boys and I were safe in our house long before dark. At my insistence Jimmy had installed three locks on each outside door of our home. While I felt secure that no intruder could get into our home, I often worried that no one could get us out in case of fire. I was caught in a circle of unhealthy fear.

Fear is a learned response. I understand the debilitating consequences of unhealthy fear. My mother was fearful and my sisters were fearful. Fear seemed to dominate all my responses to life. When I was young, my mother's father, as a practical joke, took great delight in sneaking around his grandchildren, making frightening noises. He thought it was very funny, and this set the stage for my lack of security for thirty-one years.

My earliest childhood memories of fear come from the times we spent in the pitch dark during World War II. Although we lived in Georgia, far away from the battlefront overseas, a blackout was routinely enforced in our city. During the blackout period, all lights had to be extinguished. No one was allowed on the streets except the air-raid warden. He would walk up and down the block checking all the houses.

As if it were yesterday, I remember my parents turning off all the lights and lowering the black shades at all the windows. We sat huddled in one room in total darkness and waited for the all-clear signal. I don't know how long the blackouts lasted, but it seemed like forever as we sat perfectly quiet. One of the provisions for this time spent in darkness was a small enamel potty that my mother made sure was near by. She refused to take us through the darkened house to the bathroom. This seemed to make the event even more frightening.

Of course, I don't ever recall hearing any planes fly over. I guess if that had happened as part of the test, we would have just died right there of sheer fright. I was only five, but the memory of those times produced a fear of war in my heart. My father was not fearful at all, but I never recall his doing anything to alleviate the fear that Mama was constantly instilling in us. I think perhaps he just enjoyed the total quietness of the whole procedure.

Being fearful of things in your control is one thing, but then there are circumstances totally out of your control. For instance, one afternoon several years after we were married, Jimmy told me that he and his helper had gotten the truck stuck in a bog at the head of our pond. Knowing that he had to go to work shortly, Jimmy instructed the helper to leave the truck alone, put up all the tools, and wait for his father to pick him up at about four o'clock. Then Jimmy left for work.

For some unknown reason, I decided to take the boys to visit Jimmy's mother that day. This was so unusual. We never went off in the afternoon when Jimmy went to work. I did not like coming home to a dark house. We had a nice visit and were home safely just before dark.

At six o'clock the next morning, our phone rang. A voice said, "Mrs. Camak, did my son John work yesterday?"

Right away I knew this was our helper's mother. I said, "Yes, he worked with my husband until two-thirty, and then his father picked him up."

"We don't understand," she continued. "His father came to pick him up about four and waited until five, but John was not there."

By this time Jimmy was awake. When I told him what the lady had said, Jimmy bounded out of bed, grabbed his clothes, and ran out of the door. He ran as fast as he could to the area he and John had worked the day before. Before I could get fully dressed, Jimmy ran back to our house.

"Carole, call the ambulance and the police. John is up there and he is *dead!*"

A sense of panic swept through my entire being. How could this be? I held on to Jimmy. We were both trembling.

In my desire to straighten everything out, I kept saying, "Jimmy don't worry. It will be all right."

"No, it won't be all right," Jimmy said, as if to shake reality into me. "John is up there and he is *dead.*"

When the police arrived, they determined that John had obviously tried to get the pickup truck out of the bog by himself. The tractor he used rolled back down a hill and pinned him between the door of the pickup truck and a small pine tree. Death had been instantaneous. Apparently, sometime between the time I left our house and the time his father arrived, the accident had occurred. After questioning Jimmy and then me, the police ruled the death accidental, since no one was there when it happened.

For months Jimmy and I discussed the event. The stress of the accidental death increased my fear of fate. Now I faced an enemy I could not see and certainly could not prepare for. John had disobeyed, and it cost him his life. I felt so bad. Why did I leave that afternoon? Everything seemed so strange. If only I had been there, I could have found him when his father arrived. Over and over I reasoned that if I had been home, I could have prevented his death. Of course, none of my guilty feelings were justified, but they haunted me day and night. Now I feared doing anything that could lead to another tragedy.

My life was traveling much too fast for my peace of mind. I tried unsuccessfully to talk Jimmy into selling his tractor and the truck. The constant concern that he would get hurt while working outside by himself motivated me to spend every morning outside helping him. I became his helper. The boys loved being outside with us, but through all of this, my fear increased. When Jimmy left for work, I would go inside and work until bedtime. This was too much for both of us.

Refusing to let my life's plan fall by the wayside, I tightened my grip on my little family. My recent miscarriage and the death of our young helper had created a stressful void in my life. In the hope of filling this void, my obstetrician advised me to have another baby. Jimmy and I liked the idea and thought that the obvious strain on my nerves could be eased with the anticipation of a new baby.

It is interesting how we try anything to satisfy the longing in our soul. With all the stress, fear, and uncertainties in our life, we never missed a church service. We were so faithful and presented a strong family front to all our friends at church. Without my knowing it, my family was becoming my god. I fretted over every detail, performed every duty with great care, and tried desperately to be at peace with all people. The strain was telling in my attitude of worry and in my physical exhaustion.

On March 15, 1962, we encountered another screeching halt on our out-of-control train. Just two weeks before our baby was due, I went in for my routine doctor's appointment. I noticed upon my arrival that I was greeted by the nurses and office personnel with what appeared to be extra attention. Then, without having to wait at all, I was taken directly in to see my doctor. It was unusual to move through the appointment schedule so quickly.

Dr. "B" said, "Carole, I was expecting to hear from you in the emergency room."

I was shocked. Why would he say such a thing? Then he proceeded to tell me that from the routine x-ray that had been made several weeks before, they discovered the baby I was carrying was not formed at all.

He said, "There is no bone structure. A head is visible, but the rest is a mass of unformed fetal tissue. I have been expecting your body to reject the pregnancy at any time. I do not understand why you are not having any sickness related to your condition."

What condition? I thought back to the day when the x-rays were made. One by one all the nurses and doctors had stopped by the small viewing room to see the x-ray. I had asked no questions. I marvel that I was so naive and trusting.

Obviously everyone in the office was aware of my condition. That explained the extra attention I received when I arrived. I sat stunned. How could I face another loss? What would I tell Jimmy? How could I give such bad news to our two precious little boys? They were so anxious to have a brother or a sister.

With great tenderness, Dr. "B" offered to call Jimmy.

I said, "No, just tell me what to do and I will handle it." Although I was falling apart inside, I was still holding on and trying desperately to stay in charge of our lives.

I phoned Jimmy from the waiting room. Through my tears I sobbed, "Jimmy, I need you. Meet me out front of your office. I will be there in a few minutes."

Somehow I drove the few blocks to his office, and as soon as I stopped the car, he slipped into the driver's seat.

As Jimmy drove, I told him the bad news. By then I was crying uncontrollably. The doctor had told me to go to the drugstore and get some castor oil. Jimmy went in to purchase the castor oil while I sat in the car and tried to pull myself together. I knew we would be home soon, and I could not let the boys see me so upset. Jimmy was so loving, and together we were determined to face another twist in our high-speed journey.

My instructions were to drink the castor oil, wait for the first pain, and then call the doctor. All afternoon we sat around waiting. Nothing happened. My mother, Jimmy's mother, and a friend came and waited with us. I felt like a time bomb. The suitcase was packed, and the boys were aware of some new crisis as we waited for the next event. Finally, at five-thirty, the doctor called me.

"Carole, you had better come on, and I will induce labor," he said.

Our hearts were so heavy. What was the meaning of this latest disappointment? Jimmy tried to talk positively, but I was wondering what I could have done wrong to have brought on this suffering. As we arrived at the hospital, Jimmy told me not to worry; we could always try again for another baby. At that time, that did not seem encouraging to me. I was frustrated and unsure of whether or not I could endure any more hardships.

Just before the delivery, our doctor apologized for having to tell us the bad news.

He said, "I am so sorry, but I feel you must know before going into the delivery that you will not be taking a baby home this time."

I was sedated for the delivery. Several hours later I awoke to some unbelievable news. Dr. "B" was still there. He was ecstatic.

"Congratulations, Carole, you have a fine healthy son."

"That can't be true," I said through a flood of tears. "You told me that our baby was not formed."

"I am so sorry I frightened you with such bad news. I don't know how to explain it. The x-rays revealed no bone structure at all."

Then he told me that he had consulted with four associates who had agreed with his observation when they studied my x-rays. Now, here I was with a perfectly formed baby. No one could explain what had happened.

Joy filled our hearts. We wept together and were so grateful to God for giving us this fine healthy baby.

"Please forgive me," Dr. "B" said, "for causing you and Jimmy such unnecessary grief."

Forgiving—that was the easy part. We trusted our doctor completely and knew he had only done what he felt absolutely necessary to prepare us for what he fully expected. It was sheer joy to hold this fine healthy son and know God had blessed us again.

Once again we felt we were back on track. God had blessed us as a family. Now we were puzzled as to what to name this very special gift. Every name we had talked about did not seem to fit. Jimmy went to the bookstore and bought a book of 25,000 names with their special meanings. After almost a week, he finally decided on a name. I was relieved. It was getting a little strange to hold such a special child and not even have a name for him.

"His name will be Lael Hammond Camak," he announced.

I had never heard the name Lael before. Jimmy went on to tell me that Lael means "He belongs to God." I was certainly pleased. On our drive to the hospital, Jimmy had promised God that if our baby lived, we would give it back to Him. Now the name meant even more to both of us.

From our hearts we felt sure that God had intervened in my body and that this child would be very special. Jimmy and I both thought we were Christians. After all, we were good church members. We believed in God and tried to live to please Him. We were operating on the very limited understanding of God's divine plan for our life. Little did we know that all we were doing was not what God wanted.

God is not pleased with our efforts if they are done to try to impress Him. He has a greater plan and purpose for each one of us. He wants us to belong to Him completely. Only then can we give Him first place in our hearts—no room for false gods.

Our ride of life had been very bumpy. Some of the twists and turns caused great despair and fear. At times I wanted to pull the emergency brake and get off the fast train, but now I was glad that I had held on with all my strength. Today, I know that God was holding on to me and my precious family with His strong hands.

Let's Consider the Lion of False Gods

Even the very thought of serving a false god is repulsive to most of us. For years I pictured a false god as some carved image erected by an uncivilized tribe. While attributing great power and judgment to a lifeless object, the worshipers tremble for fear of displeasing the gods they serve. In reality false gods are not limited to people in other countries. When we face and identify the lion of false gods, we will recognize that they are the familiar areas of pride, pleasure, and success. False gods can be beautiful in their own right but deadly when they rule our thoughts and activities.

The desire to control is generally the foundation stone for erecting a false god. Most of us struggle with control. Even the weakest individual likes to think he is in control of his life. It is difficult to cope when unexplained events like accidents and failures occur. When we feel insecure and lack confidence, we desperately display an attitude of being on top of the situation by assuming control.

No one sets out to erect a false god. By simply focusing our attention on anyone or anything, we unconsciously begin to protect and worship people, goals, and dreams. False gods are not hideous in nature. Seldom are they carved in stone or elaborately covered with fine gold. In fact, all to often they are members of our family. A special gift or ability can assume first place in our life and become a false god. They slide undetected into first place in our hearts.

So, how do I relinquish control without becoming a wimp? Once I identify a false god, what action can I take to destroy its power over my life? In Proverbs 3:5–6 we find the solution: "Trust in the Lord with all your heart and lean not on your own understanding; in all your ways acknowledge Him, and He will make your paths straight."

To trust means to rely on and to have full confidence in a person or an object. We find it difficult to trust many people. But when we know that God loves us and has our best interest at heart, trust comes easier. In short, trust means I allow Him to be in control of my life. My own understanding is limited, but His is perfect.

When I acknowledge God in every detail of my life, He is able to direct my life in the best possible way. There is nothing in my life that He is not interested in. As I acknowledge all my ways before Him, I find new insights and gain a clearer perspective on the importance of each decision I must make.

This does not mean I send my brain or common sense on vacation. I can effectively make daily judgments based on a revelation of His divine will in my life. God will instruct us through His Word, through circumstances, and also through wise counselors He sends our way.

There can only be one commander and chief at any given time. Jesus was asked to identify the greatest commandment of all. In Mark 12:30 Jesus answered by giving to those Pharisees, as well as to us, the secret of contentment: "Love the Lord your God with all your heart and with all your soul and with all your mind and with all your strength: this is the first commandment."

How often we place family members, children, or perhaps our own goals ahead of the Lord our God. These things can become the gods of our life if we are not careful. There is no place in our lives for false gods. God must be first in our worship and first in our heart.

What about you? What is first in your life? Are you willing to tear down the false gods that have slipped into your life? Do you make out your list of priorities and then ask God to bless it? Or, are you willing to sign a blank sheet of paper and allow God to fill in the list as He sees fit? True freedom can come only when we let God be first in our lives.

Perhaps it is time to surrender to the one who created you and longs to be your One True God.

CHAPTER 5

⹂ↄℭ

FROM MAKE-BELIEVE TO REALITY

We live in a game-playing society. There are games to entertain and games to challenge. Some are designed for fun while others provoke fierce competition. From entertainment parks to educational seminars, simulators create the sensation of functioning in a real-life experience.

Once, while visiting a theme park, Jimmy and I stood in line for an hour in order to participate in a "Back to the Future" ride. Approaching the door of the realistic car, the attendant on duty instructed us to store our video camera bag on the shelf close by.

Jimmy said, "Are you sure we will come back to this same spot?"

"Oh yes," the attendant replied, "you will be right here when the ride is over."

Once the door of our car closed, the lights went out and the dashboard lit up to reveal the dials of a race car driver's dream. Abruptly the car began to move from side to side. As the sound of the motor roared, we were traveling back to the future with the same characters from the movie.

At the end of the journey the door locks snapped open and we stepped out of the car. Sure enough, there was Jimmy's camera bag—exactly where he had placed it before our exciting adventure. We had experienced the ride of a lifetime without ever having left our little cubicle.

In life we often enter a land of make-believe that makes distinguishing fantasy from reality quite difficult. I wonder sometimes if that is not a common problem. The false looks so real that we are deceived into playing a game instead of living life the way it was meant to be.

In any game it is important to know the rules. In the game of life we learn the rules by just observing another player; then without questioning, we often join right in and adapt our own life pattern to someone's personalized rules. One generation plays a game and then unknowingly passes the pattern down to the next generation. The game remains the same unless the rules are questioned. Then, much to our surprise, the make-believe gives way to reality.

Let me give you an example of what I mean from my own life experience. My mother, Eleanor, was a very fearful person. Her constant unseen companion was the lion of fear. Just as a lion in the jungle may at first appear uninterested and then suddenly spring into action, my mother's fear was capable of coming to life at a moment's notice. Everyone knew that she was very uncomfortable in the dark and was almost petrified in a storm. The common-sense precautions issued by the weather bureau were not enough for us. My mother's idea of safety involved gathering in a huddle on the sofa, covering up with a blanket, and waiting for the storm to cease. The heat was intense, but we did not care. At least we felt secure. Because we saw fear as such a controlling emotion, my sisters and I felt justified in our fear.

One evening the lion of fear met the lion tamer. When Jamey and Jody were preschoolers, Jimmy and I went to visit my parents. A summer thunderstorm arose and before I knew what was happening, my two sons were huddled in my lap. My mother, my sister, and I were also visibly frightened by the storm, and my sons picked up on my fear. We were in no immediate danger, but out of habit we experienced this natural response to any storm.

"What are you all afraid of?" Jimmy asked.

"The storm, of course," was my reply.

He could not believe what he was seeing. The fear I had grown up with was being handed down to another generation. Of course, I had never instructed the children on how to be afraid; observation was their teacher. Children learn what they live with.

"Come on, Carole, get the boys," Jimmy said. "We are going home."

My mother thought Jimmy had lost his mind. Who would go out in such a bad storm? She reminded us that we could all be struck by lightening. My mother was furious with Jimmy. To think he would risk our lives by insisting on leaving during such a frightening time was a preposterous notion.

Something in his tone of voice let me know he meant business, so I gathered up our sons and made a quick dash out in the rain to our car. The boys were crying, and I did not understand his urgent need to leave.

When we came to the end of the driveway, Jimmy turned in the opposite direction of our house.

"Where are you going?" I said.

"We are going to take a ride and watch the storm," Jimmy answered with a calm voice.

I thought that my mother was right. He was out of his mind. I wondered why he was behaving so foolishly. Didn't he realize how dangerous a storm could be?

We rode for several miles into town and down the main street of the business area. In a calm voice he talked about the need to have a healthy respect for lightening. But then he began to describe the wonder of such a beautiful display of nature. The boys listened with new interest. I had never heard that approach. All my life I had heard about the unpredictable power of lightening— stories about the time a bolt of lightening had traveled through the room of my great-aunt's house and killed her two large dogs asleep on the floor.

Finally, he said, "Jamey and Jody, I want you to let me know the next lightening flash you see and the next roll of thunder you hear."

"What a ridiculous game," I thought.

With wide eyes of expectancy, they leaned closer to the back windows. They were busy looking and listening. I suddenly realized that they were not afraid anymore.

"I saw it, Daddy! I heard the thunder," Jamey shouted with excitement.

"Me too." said Jody.

Jimmy reached into his pocket and gave each boy a nickel. They were overjoyed. With great enthusiasm they both continued to watch the sky. Each time the boys spied lightening, Jimmy dropped another nickel into their anxious hands. When each one had about fifty cents, Jimmy turned the car toward home. To my knowledge, from that night to this, the boys have never been afraid of storms. The rules of the game had been changed. One unhealthy fear that had long crippled my life was broken.

I was beginning to learn that just because you have been taught by example to play the game of life by someone's preconceived rules, the rules can be changed. I certainly did not want my sons to live in the fear I had lived in for so long. This was just the beginning of my willingness to examine the rules of the game for my own life.

Early the next morning I called my mother, thinking that she would be pleased to hear that her grandsons were not afraid anymore. I told her about Jimmy's lesson.

"Well, I hope Jimmy has a lot of money. If he is going to pay them a nickel every time it thunders, he will soon go broke," she said bitterly.

"Jimmy is not going to continue paying them a nickel. He just wanted them to develop a healthy respect for a storm but not live with the unhealthy fear that I have grown up with," I replied.

My explanation fell on deaf ears. Jimmy was very foolish to take us out in the storm, she protested. While I could not understand her reasoning, I knew that if we were going to teach our children anything that differed from my mother's beliefs, we were in for a rough ride of criticism. I was discovering that my husband had strengths to help me in my areas of weaknesses. My boys had been set free from the fear of storms. I felt a sense of wonder to see how differently I felt about storms.

In order to accept change, we have to be ready to see our own weaknesses. Often we become so familiar with a certain lifestyle that we cannot comprehend anything else.

With a strong desire to build a good family, I was open to learning. This meant I had to listen to instruction and be willing to make necessary adjustments. In Proverbs 18 I read, "The heart of the discerning acquires knowledge; the ears of the wise seek it out."

Two things that aid in growth are: (1) a teachable spirit and (2) an attitude of seeking truth. How often I have found that a story sounds good until it is questioned. For instance, until I was exposed to a healthy respect for storms, I lived under an unhealthy fear. It produced anxiety and bondage. When I saw the fear of storms broken, I wondered what other lions were lurking in the shadows.

The wind of change was blowing, and I liked the refreshing relief. Change doesn't occur overnight. It takes time and a lot of give and take. I liked the strength I saw in Jimmy. I found myself wanting to take a closer look at my life.

The rules of the game were so established in my life that I was unaware I was playing "Let's pretend." We attended every single meeting at church. Because I felt uneasy about leaving my children in the nursery, they sat with me in every service. I truly felt any mother "worth her salt," so to speak, should be able to control her own children. Common sense convinced me that they would be safer with me than back in some nursery room.

My boys never talked in church, drew on any bulletins, or misbehaved. If they even looked restless, I would reach down and pinch their little legs really hard.

Then, if they tried to cry, I would lean down and whisper, "If you don't behave, I will take you out and tear you up."

Proud that I had gained complete control over them, I would promptly sit up straight and smile as if everything was fine. No one knew what went on with my children in church except me and the boys. They knew better than to say anything. For some reason, they never wanted to wear short pants to church.

Upon leaving the service, someone would always pat me on the back and say, "Carole, it just does my heart good to see your precious little Christian family in church."

How sad. We were there all right. My children were never sick enough to stay home on Sunday or Wednesday nights. I felt we had to be there in perfect attendance. We even shared their mumps and chicken pox at Sunday school. After all, I had been taught that church attendance was absolutely necessary if you were going to please God.

The "Let's pretend" game can last only so long. Sooner or later you must come to the finish line and face reality. Until this time I had been steadily moving on an escalator higher and higher to achieve all my goals, but soon I began a downward spiral that would cause me to closely examine the fantasy I called home.

I possessed a strong need to be the self-protector of my little family. Obviously, the lion of fear I had grown up with was waiting for the right occasion to claim its prey. Perfect behavior in church was one thing I could handle myself, but fear of fate was a powerful lion. With all my protective will, I had no way of controlling circumstances. There was no obvious cause to worry, but the "what if" mentality became my overriding master. The occasional reports I heard of accidents at the school grounds or runaway vehicles that caused traffic accidents produced in me an unhealthy fear.

I became aware of my children losing my protective care when Jamey was old enough to go to kindergarten. Of course, not any kindergarten would do. I chose a well-established kindergarten under the direction of the mother of a schoolmate of mine. Since this lady had been director for twenty years, she would surely know all the safe things to do.

When the big day for fall registration arrived, Jamey, who was then five, and I entered the kindergarten room together, hand in hand. He was excited, but I was very tense. The teacher carefully gave me all the customary instructions. Then she shocked me into reality.

"You are so fortunate to live in this neighborhood," she said. "You will be able to be in a super car pool."

She saw my worried expression. "Is anything wrong?" she asked.

"I will not be putting my son in a car pool," I said. "What kind of a mother do you think I am? I don't know how those other women drive. They may not drive carefully. Who knows what could happen to my child if he rides with someone I don't know?"

"Well, bless your heart, honey," she said. "If that is the way you feel, you just bring him yourself."

"I certainly will," I replied. "That is my responsibility as his mother."

That was a very difficult year and proved to be the catalyst for more stress for me. At the beginning of the school year, I discovered that my handpicked kindergarten director decided to retire. I was devastated. It was too late to back out now, so I began driving Jamey to kindergarten every morning at nine and returning for him at twelve. I had three good, solid hours to stay at home and worry. I did not like anyone who suggested that I might be overprotective. I felt a mother was supposed to be like a mother hen, always hovering over her brood.

I thought I had handled the fearful lion of fate by meeting each circumstance head on. Then, unexpectedly, I was shocked to encounter another lion that threatened our personal safety. This time it was associated with a national enemy. Following World War II, nuclear reactors were designed to provide neutrons to produce plutonium, an explosive catalyst used in atomic bombs. The US Atomic Energy Commission established a reactor near Aiken, South Carolina, capable of manufacturing large quantities of plutonium each year. This plant provided many local jobs for our area in construction and operations. The local people referred to it as "the bomb plant."

As a child I had heard our pastor preach many messages on the possibility of a great atomic bomb that was being perfected at that time. Again and again he reminded us that it could easily be dropped on America. He used graphic word pictures for the result of such a bomb, and I lived in fear of some other country taking aim at us. The atomic bomb would be deadly. There would be little warning and almost no survivors.

Knowing that the Savannah River Reactor was located just thirty miles from our home made me very uneasy. Everyone knew that a key component necessary for the making of the atomic bomb was produced there. Naturally, security was tight. I felt certain Russia had our area at the top of their priority list of cities to annihilate.

Panic was the order of my life. With a simple electrical power failure, I became hysterical. The additional responsibility of safety for our children increased my fear. I not only had to look out for my safety, but I had to make sure our children were protected.

Like putting on a blindfold and hoping the danger would go away, I refused to listen to any news reports. My imagination worked overtime. I chose not to be informed of things I could not control, especially when they only made me more fearful. Every evening Jimmy would watch the news on television. Assuming that what I didn't know couldn't hurt me, I always made a point of finding something to keep me occupied in another part of the house.

One evening Jimmy and his friend Ed were watching a special about the building of the Berlin Wall. Jimmy insisted that I watch this moment in history. I was panic stricken. If East and West Germany could be divided with a wall of barbed wire and concrete blocks, what would keep the same thing from happening in our land? I was consumed by paranoia.

After the report, Jimmy and Ed discussed the precarious situation of our world. They had attended an investment meeting earlier that evening and discussed what possible effect the Berlin Wall had on our economy. Although Ed was a senior research physicist at the Savannah River Plant, he seemed to be more interested in the financial aspect of this crisis than any imminent danger. Their response seemed strange to me. When Jimmy decided it was time for him to drive Ed home, one mile away, neither one of them noticed that I was on the verge of hysteria.

"Carole," Ed said as he walked out of our door, "how good are you at digging?"

I thought that was a curious question.

I answered, "Digging what?"

"A fallout shelter," he said jokingly. "It looks like we are going to have to construct one if we plan to survive an atomic bomb attack."

I was so frightened. This was no joke to me. I was familiar with the layout of a fallout shelter—small and gloomy. I could not comprehend trying to survive in such cramped conditions. How could we have one large enough for our family and my parents? My mind flooded with one question after the other.

The fear was overwhelming. I wanted desperately to go to sleep in the hope that this was just a bad dream. In my desperation I remembered an old-time remedy that might work. My parents were not drinkers of alcoholic beverages, but in our home there had always been a fifth of whiskey stored away for medicinal purposes. Since my father had given Jimmy a bottle to keep on hand, I knew just what I could do.

I knew one small drink would put me to sleep immediately. I went to the kitchen, poured a little Coca-Cola in a glass and added a good portion of whisky. Apparently my portions were reversed. I must have used more whisky than Coca-Cola. I went straight to bed and was in a deep sleep in a matter of minutes.

The next thing I knew, I awoke to hear someone laughing. When I opened my eyes, Jimmy was standing by our bed. He was holding his side and doubled over in laughter. I was angry. Why did he wake me up?

"Carole, what have you done?" he asked. "You smell like a brewery!"

"I just fixed myself a little drink so I could go to sleep fast," I said. "Jimmy, I am so scared that we are all going to die."

After he finally stopped laughing, he assured me that everything would be all right and that he would take care of me. I never tried that little remedy again. I was so ashamed, but I had had nowhere else to turn—the fear did not go away. With a husband who loved me unconditionally and three healthy children, I should have been able to face each day with joy. Instead, I lived from day to day in fear of life and death. During all this time, no one ever knew about my overwhelming fear. I hid it very well. People judged me by what they saw on the outside. My mask of contentment hid my fear from those in my close circle.

By denial and calculated efforts, I was able to handle the lions of fear of storms, foreign enemies, and fate, but then I came face to face with the lion that surrounded me daily—the fear of people. This fear crippled my participation outside of my immediate family. No one knew how threatening outsiders were to my peace of mind. Most of the ladies at church thought I was snooty. They assumed that I felt superior to them since I would not associate with anyone but my mother and her close friend, Clara. I had no friends my own age. No one realized that I was frightened to be anywhere without my mother. Since she went to all the church meetings, I always had a companion. On the rare occasions when she was ill and could not go, I missed the meeting also, under the guise of taking care of her.

I felt inferior to anyone who could do anything I could not do. The thought of making crafts made me feel very insecure. In recent years I have learned that some people make crafts and other people buy them. The people who invest time and money making crafts love people like me who buy them.

One day while Jimmy sat at home with a broken leg, I had to go to the bank for him. It was awful. I finished my business at the teller window and promptly retreated to my car. The tears flowed hot and heavy. Professional people and clerks made me feel very uneasy. It was much easier to play by my own narrow rules and live isolated from others who would be a threat to my peace of mind.

"Why do I feel so inferior to people? If only I could be free," I thought.

I was comfortable with isolation until another threat came from the outside. A special news bulletin flashed on the television, and I fell apart emotionally. President John F. Kennedy announced that a blockade had been put in place to stop Russian ships from going to Cuba. Closer and closer it came. Now the Russians were in Cuba. It was easy to see that any missiles in Cuba that were aimed at Florida could easily reach Georgia. "We are doomed," I thought.

Anytime now we could be under attack. In desperation, I called my mother's home. She did not answer. Where could she be? I suddenly felt abandoned. Jimmy was at work. With a sense of urgency to stock up on food in case of an attack, there was only one thing left to do. I had to go to the grocery store immediately, and I had no choice but to go alone. Rapidly, I pushed a grocery cart up and down the aisles. In a state of panic, I filled my cart with powdered milk, peanut butter, dry cereal, instant oatmeal, and other provisions. By the time I had finished, $150 worth of necessary supplies were bagged and in my car. After all, it was my responsibility to feed and provide for my children. I hurried home and quickly stocked the shelves of a walk-in closet in our basement. Someone could have easily done his or her grocery shopping in my basement.

That was just the beginning. Several days later when the anticipated attack had not occurred, I convinced Jimmy to take me to a wholesale grocery house to buy cases of canned goods. Bottles of water were carefully placed in the basement closet and blankets stacked neatly in the corner. I was ready physically but falling apart emotionally.

One day Jimmy said, "Carole, I think you have a problem."

At first I was angry. I said, "You bet I have a problem. We have three small children, the whole world is falling apart, and who knows what will come next."

"I think you have a problem that is larger than all of that. Your fear of everything is starting to control your whole life," he said.

He was right of course. He lived so close to my problem that he could make a very clear observation of just how much fear was ruling my life. All of my efforts to be the best wife, mother, and daughter were demanding every ounce of effort in me. No matter what I did, I felt guilty all the time. How could I be all things to all people? It was becoming apparent that I could not handle myself or my fears.

My escalator was going down, down, down. The games were no longer working and I was getting very frustrated. It was easy to see that my life was not my own. Because my mother was so possessive of my time, she always required an account of everything I did. With no apology, she let me know when she did not approve of my decisions. Then more guilt. I secretly felt resentment and anger. Certainly I could not tell anyone how I really felt. Least of all could I tell Mama. So the game continued.

I loved my mother, but I was beginning to see that my life was full of torment because of many of the pressures she applied. I was fearful of the future. I felt guilty for not pleasing everyone. And I was beginning to question my own self-worth. The threat of death hung over me all the time.

During this downward spiral, we kept up the good appearance of a family. We never missed a church service. I was surrounded by people in church who had known me since childhood, yet no one ever told me that God loved me and had a wonderful plan for my life. In fact, I did not know my life was a farce, because it seemed no different from the lives of other people in my church.

Jimmy was a very wise husband. He could see the intense pressure I was under and suggested that we might need to make a move away from the house we both loved so much. He could see my total dependence upon Mama, as well as my fear of disappointing her. Jimmy had always operated under the belief that we all have three choices when facing a problem. We can correct it, live with it, or move away from it. He had tried to correct the problem I was dealing with and could not. Then he thought we could just learn to cope with it, but he soon observed that my personal bondage was taking too great a toll on me. So he decided we should move. Although it was difficult for me, I did recognize that perhaps a move would help me stand on my own for a change.

We purchased a lot in a beautiful new subdivision. We would be about seven miles away from my parent's home. The prospects of building a new home took my mind off the fear. I told myself that our children needed to live in a nice neighborhood. When I shared our plans, Mama was angry.

"Why are you moving? We sold you our pond and eight acres to build your house on. Are you not happy there? How could you move away? We thought you would live there forever," she said.

More guilt dumped on me. My parents blamed Jimmy for making me move. Jimmy did not mind. He knew that the move was in my best interest. He reminded them that when he bought the land eight years ago and built our house, Daddy had assured him no strings were attached. It would be his land to do with as he saw fit. Those words sounded good, but were not necessarily true. Another valuable lesson learned the hard way.

As we began to build the new house, the excitement grew. Each boy would have his own room. The house was well suited to our growing needs. Mama and Daddy would have nothing to do with any of our plans. They did not even come by to see the progress. I was torn between the excitement my family felt and my efforts to keep peace with my parents. The boys could not understand why their grandparents were keeping such a distance from us. I was confused. Trying to keep up all the appearances of acceptance, I filled my days with preparation for the move and refused to think about my emotional hurt.

After a strong push to get in by Christmas, we made the move on Saturday, December 20. What a busy day. Mama and Daddy offered no help. I was determined to be happy even though my heart was breaking. Surely they would soften their attitudes soon. I constantly searched my mind to make sure I had done nothing wrong. Jimmy got a little frustrated with me and kept telling me that although we loved my parents, we had our lives to live also.

Early the next morning Jimmy awoke to find that I had already slipped out of bed. When he came downstairs, he found me out in the garage looking through a chest of drawers that held Lael's clothes.

"Carole, what are you doing?"

"Today is Sunday," I replied. "I am looking for some clothes for Lael to wear to church."

"I am exhausted. We went to bed last night after midnight. Can't we please miss church this one morning?" Jimmy asked, almost in a pleading tone of voice.

"No! How can we stay at home?" I asked. "Just look around you at how God has blessed us. It is certainly not too much to ask us to go to church for Him, is it?"

"Okay, we will go," Jimmy said. "I know you would have too much to explain to your mother if you didn't go."

That hurt my feelings, but I knew he was right. At this point, I certainly did not want to cross my mother again. Two days later our Christmas tree was up and fully decorated. On Christmas Day I cooked a traditional Christmas dinner. Mama and Daddy did not come to visit. When I called, my father said, "Your mother is sick and we are not coming over."

We went over to see them in the afternoon. Mama was in the bed. She did not have a cold. She could not explain how she felt, but I do believe it was a result of the stress that was controlling her life also. I felt as if I were being punished for moving.

Determined to start a new life for our family, I mustered up my courage and visited my new neighbors. Since I had never lived in a neighborhood before, I was totally unprepared for the differences I found in families that looked like us on the outside but were obviously different. After a little conversation, I felt totally inferior to the very ladies I had hoped would be my new friends. They talked of playing golf, bridge clubs, and their memberships in their garden club. I could not play golf. The only card game I had ever played was "Go Fish," so I knew I would not be comfortable with these ladies. I was familiar with garden work, but somehow that was not the kind of garden these ladies talked about.

I know today that the feelings of inferiority that I lived with were no one's fault but mine. The ladies were very nice. It was a matter of my projecting my insecurity into every encounter. They had no idea how I perceived our relationship. Each neighbor was busy building her own life.

I began, again, questioning myself. Had I made a mistake in leaving my mother's close companionship? Would I be able to find my complete fulfillment in my own family without any outside input from others? Although I never talked to anyone about my fears, I had observed that most people did not seem to be bothered by fear at all. Perhaps they were playing a more convincing game than I was. As I became aware that my sons were developing their individual personalities, I worried that they might grow up to feel the insecurity I had felt for so many years.

My fantasy life was coming up short, and I desperately needed to find some sense of direction for my life. But how could I distinguish between make-believe and reality?

Is there a place where fantasy ends and reality begins? Yes, fantasy should be limited to theme parks and perhaps childhood stories. But reality is facing each day with confidence and recognizing who you are. It is a keen awareness of life as it ought to be according to God's rule book—the Bible.

Let's Consider the Lion of Fear

If I had to identify the most powerful lion of my life, it would certainly be the lion of fear. Just as the lion, a large, powerful member of the cat family, is commonly referred to as "the king of the beasts," the ever-present lion of fear was the king of my emotions. Fear is a real emotion that has the ability to create great stress in an instant. It is a feeling of anxiety and agitation brought on by the presence or nearness of danger. The threat of danger is often only imaginary, but its effect is still debilitating. The bitter fruit of timidity, apprehension, and even terror creates the inability to cope with the present circumstances of life.

There is a story told about the first Earl of Burma. His name was Louis Mountbatten. At the age of five, he was reluctant to go up to bed alone in the dark.

"It isn't the darkness," he told his father confidentially, "there are wolves up there!"

His father smiled. "There are no wolves in this house," he said reassuringly.

This was of little consolation to the rational young Mountbatten.

"I dare say there aren't," he replied, "but I *think* there are."

Fear is not all bad. You would probably agree that we should have a healthy fear of rattlesnakes, weapons of destruction, and even some out-of-control people. But an unhealthy fear that keeps you from enjoying daily life must be addressed and dealt with conclusively. To gain victory, we must be able to distinguish the difference between make-believe fear and justifiable fear. Only then will we become mature and productive individuals.

Everyone agrees that unhealthy fear is damaging to our peace of mind and crippling to our happiness. So where does fear come from? Fear is a learned response. Psychologists have concluded that a baby is born with only one fear—the fear of falling. As we get older, a more common name for fear is worry. Even if you have never properly identified fear in your life, you probably would agree that you occasionally engage in worry. We all know how useless worry is. Even a brief reading of God's Word will reveal a multitude of verses that begin with *Fear not*. Good advice, no doubt. So what is the opposite of fear? It is faith. Sounds simple enough, but what is faith? Is it something you can see? Can anyone have faith? How does it develop? Volumes have been written explaining faith. Highly educated scholars have spent hours expounding the importance of faith. But I like to think of faith in the simple definition I heard from a precious old saint who lived a life full of faith.

His comment: "To me, faith is the hook that you confidently hang your life on."

For faith to be active it must have an object. In Hebrews 12:2 I read that we are to keep our eyes on Jesus, the author and perfecter of our faith. "Now faith is being sure of what we hope for and certain of what we do not see" (Hebrews 11:1). That means God, who is the creator of the entire universe, can be trusted. From past experiences, I can be sure He will do what He says He will do. My part is to trust His unchanging nature and His unfailing love.

By faith I have learned to enjoy the summer storms as a display of the awesome power of nature. With proper respect for lightening and taking the necessary precautions for safety, I refuse to be bound by the fear that once held me captive. By faith, I no longer fear fate. To a great extent, my future is out of my control. I choose to rely on God's knowledge of my need and His love toward me instead of my puny understanding of what I think I need. The "what if" mentality has been replaced with the confidence that nothing can separate me from His love. So why should I worry? It has been determined that nine out of the ten things we worry about never happen; think of all that wasted energy and time.

Last but not least, I am no longer intimidated by people. My fingerprints remind me that I am one of a kind. That sets me free to enjoy being me. God loves me! That is more important than all the acceptance by my peers. No one is without special abilities and gifts. Beginning with the precious gift of life, we need to discover our gifts and use them for the glory and honor of God.

Life can be a jungle. Lions of fear may abide in many areas of our lives. What about your life? Does the lion of fear crouch in the shadows of your thoughts and plans? Are you living below the poverty level spiritually? If you are looking for a simple method to develop faith, why not begin with this three-step plan of action that I used to find freedom. First, ask God to reveal to you the fear that binds your mind. Next, seek to understand His design for your life. Then, knock at the door of trust, and it will be opened to you. Step by step you will begin to walk by faith, and wholeness will be yours.

"Fear knocked at the door—faith answered and found no one there!"

CHAPTER 6

ᎶᏍᎥᎥᏅᏒ

LOOKING FOR LOVE IN
ALL THE WRONG PLACES

L ife is like a maze—an intricate network of winding path-ways. Anyone can begin the journey, but it is important to be on the correct path if you plan to reach the intended exit point. Perhaps that is a clue. We get too busy with activity and refuse to admit that there is a right and a wrong choice.

As a young mother of three healthy sons, my energy level was stretched to capacity. Days were consumed with school activities, Cub Scouts, and swimming lessons. With all my housekeeping chores added, the list seemed to require more time than I could find. By evening I was exhausted. In fact, I get weary today just thinking about all the hats I attempted to wear. It is real work trying to be "Supermom."

I can't help chuckling when someone asks a stay-at-home mom if she works. What a ridiculous question. Anyone who has tried to balance the care of children, the management of a home, the preparation of meals, and the scheduling of appointments while still remaining sane can testify to full knowledge of work.

A friend of mine used to say, "I just get up in the morning, try to keep things from falling apart, and go to bed at night to rest for the next day." She was obviously caught in a life that could be described as a rut. You know what a rut is, don't you? Someone defined it for me: A rut is a grave with both ends open.

When I think of my experience on a moving sidewalk in the Atlanta airport, I remember what a welcome relief it was. Having traveled on a fast rain, two escalators, and what seemed like miles of speed walking, just standing on the motorized sidewalk seemed to be the perfect break I needed. Watching other passengers pass me by, I wondered why they were in such a rush. Where could they possibly be going at such a fast pace? It was much easier to just relax and let the sidewalk do the walking.

Perhaps this is an appropriate picture of life. It is easy to stand to the side and let life happen. We feel very relaxed and unthreatened until we become aware that others are moving out faster and with greater confidence. With little concern of the destination others were pursuing, I found myself caught up in the hustle and bustle of living.

One day I complained to our pediatrician about all I had to do to keep up with three active boys. As the father of ten children, his answer came readily from his years of experience.

"Carole, you will know your family is large enough when you have something going on all the time," he said. "Just when you get one child well, another one breaks an arm or comes down with a childhood disease. So just try to relax and let life happen."

Let life happen? I knew what he was talking about. Already, without any effort on my part, we seemed to be going from one disaster to another. Believing that each problem developed from some failure on my part to be in control, I took everything personally. I began to examine my destination. Could I be caught in a rut? What were my intended goals?

I struggled to find contentment in all my material things. Compared to the limited resources of my childhood years, I was rich. God had abundantly blessed me with a husband who loved me and three healthy children, but I was unaware of the lion of barrenness slinking nearby, keeping close tabs on my "accumulated stuff." Everything seemed to be working out better than I had even dreamed. What could possibly go wrong? I just needed to relax and be satisfied.

It was spring of 1965, and I was hoping for some relief from the pressures that seemed to be engulfing my life. It had been a difficult few months since our move into our new home. I had struggled with a bout of the flu. Also, during this time, we had Jimmy's fifteen-year-old half-brother staying with us while their mother, Opal, was having surgery. I was physically weak and mentally tired. Then, during my routine visit to my gynecologist, I was given some rather shocking news: I was pregnant! Another baby was due to arrive in November. My weakened physical condition, coupled with the realization that this was not something I'd planned, made me cry. Just when I thought I might have some time for myself, we would be starting all over.

Driving home, I wondered what Jimmy's reaction would be. Would he be excited or disappointed? He enjoyed our family and had never expressed any reluctance to have more children. Anxiously I prepared a special dinner and waited for his arrival. As soon as I told him my news, all my fears were relieved. Jimmy was overjoyed.

The following Tuesday was Ladies Aid meeting at the church. Every month I attended with my mother. All of the other ladies were her age, but they welcomed me warmly as their only young member. Choosing to miss this meeting, I braced myself for the phone call I knew would come. Sure enough, just before dinner, Mama called.

"Why didn't you come to the meeting today?" she asked.

"I didn't feel like it," I said nervously. "You know I haven't recovered fully from the flu, so I just stayed home today to rest."

I secretly hoped that would be the end of the questions.

"Oh," she said with an audible sigh of relief. "I am glad that it is just the flu. I was so afraid there was something else wrong with you."

I felt this was her way of saying, "I was afraid you were pregnant." From my experience with Mama, I knew that she adored babies. She would tenderly hold and love anyone's infant, yet she always seemed angry whenever she heard anyone was pregnant. If I could only understand her apparent bitterness. What experience in her past could possibly cause her to act so negatively?

I knew I would have to tell her sooner or later, so I cleared my throat and decided now was the time. Talking to her on the phone and not face to face helped me respond with unaccustomed boldness.

"Mama, there is nothing wrong with me," I said in a very confident manner. "In fact everything is just right. In November we are going to have another baby."

Trying to sound calm, I talked about how thrilled Jimmy and I were at the prospect of this new addition to our family. Then, as if to build my case even stronger, I told her that this baby would not be a financial hardship and that there was no reason not to be excited. Nothing in my previous experience prepared me for her reaction. She hit the ceiling.

"Well, you can have this baby if you want," she said, her voice straining to a higher tone. "I won't care if it is a little boy or a little girl—I will not love it! You can know one thing right now: I don't intend to have anything to do with this baby."

I was angry. For a few moments I did not know how to respond, but then I found the words.

"Mama, if that is how you feel, that is your choice," I said. "But we will love this baby enough for all of us, and it will be your loss if you choose to act this way."

We ended the conversation, but it wasn't over. Mama kept her distance from us. She refused to visit in our home and was very cold toward me and the children when we met at church. The boys could not understand why she acted coldly when they tried to hug her at church, and I did not know how to explain it to them.

At first I felt deeply, personally hurt. Then, as if I had been disobedient or defiant, I felt guilty about my pregnancy. I searched every memory trying desperately to understand her behavior. It left me puzzled. Why was she so bitter? She had always loved babies. What could possibly be her reason for rejecting my unborn baby?

That summer Jimmy and I kept very busy. We were preparing for our baby's arrival while enjoying our three sons. My parents never showed any interest in our lives and ignored my pregnancy as if it were not real.

In the predawn hours of October 9, 1965, I went into premature labor. Jimmy called our neighbor, Joyce, and asked her to stay with our children while he took me to the hospital.

Although the labor had begun a month early, the delivery was imminent. Our fourth son arrived shortly after one on that Saturday afternoon. Jimmy was elated. While I slept soundly, he hurried home to share the good news of a baby brother with Jamey, Jody, and Lael. Surely nothing could spoil our family's happiness now.

Around six that evening, I awoke to hear the exciting news of the premature but safe birth of our son. On the way to my private room, the nurse wheeled me by the nursery. For a few short moments I had the joy of viewing the very newest Camak. He looked so small. He weighed only five pounds. I was concerned that he might have to stay longer in the hospital. Quickly the nurse assured me he had been examined by the pediatrician and everything seemed fine. A sense of relief filled my heart.

As the nurse held him, I noticed a difference in his breathing. Each time he exhaled, his little chest seemed to sink in like a deep cavity. When I asked her why this was happening, she explained that it was possibly due to the position she was holding him in. Then as she lowered him into her arms like a newborn, his breathing appeared normal. I dismissed my concern.

Soon Jimmy arrived. Carrying handwritten congratulations cards from each of our sons, he was overflowing with their exciting comments about the new baby brother. I then shared with

Jimmy my concern for our baby's breathing, and he responded like a protective father, offering to call the pediatrician right away. Perhaps the doctor needed to check our son again, he suggested.

"No need to bother him," I said. "He has already checked him. Surely if there is any problem, the night nurse will notify him."

Because I was still very groggy from the delivery, Jimmy let me sleep and left to pick up our sons from the neighbor's house. I slept well all night. At 6 a.m., I was awakened by the cry of hungry newborns being brought to their mothers. I waited for my son, but no one brought him.

Breakfast came, but I could not eat. I began to cry. A senior nursing student came bouncing into my room. Immediately she noticed my tears.

"What is wrong?" she asked.

"Something must be wrong with my baby," I sobbed tearfully. "No one brought him to me all night. I hear the other babies being brought from the nursery, but I have only a breakfast tray."

"Wait just one minute," the nursing student said as she bounded out of my room. Within minutes she appeared with a big smile on her face.

"I saw Baby Camak and he is fine," she said enthusiastically. "He has ten fingers and ten toes and a nose right in the middle of his face. He looks perfect to me," she said, trying desperately to relieve my fears.

Less than thirty minutes later the pediatrician arrived at my room. He introduced himself to me.

"Mrs. Camak," he said, "I need to talk with you and your husband right away."

I explained that Jimmy was planning to take our sons to his mother's house to spend Sunday afternoon, and he would be at the hospital around two.

"Perhaps you don't understand," he said in a much stronger tone of voice. "We have a crisis! I need to talk with both parents immediately!"

I did not need any further convincing. When I called home and told Jimmy about the urgency of the doctor's request, he agreed to come right away. Alone in my hospital room, my imagination began to race away. What could be wrong? Our baby had passed the weight problem, the nurse said he was fine, but something was obviously creating serious concern. Instantly, the mental picture of his labored breathing loomed in my mind.

After what seemed like hours but was only minutes, Jimmy arrived. No longer alone, I felt sure everything would be all right. Then the doctor told us that our baby was in critical condition. He had developed a hyaline membrane around his lungs, and his breathing was extremely difficult. Then the doctor told us that a mistake had been made in the nursery—life saving treatment had been delayed because the night nurse had chosen to hold and rock our son instead of alerting the doctor to the obvious change in his ability to breathe on his own. I was horrified.

"We are doing all we can to help him," he said. "He is a fighter, but even with our best medical care, he may not be strong enough to overcome this setback."

The critical time would be seventy-two hours. We suddenly felt alone and frightened. Facing the possible death of our son, I did not know how to handle it. This was an emergency. The only thing I could do was to pray. But how do you pray when your heart is breaking? What could I say to God that would let Him know how I felt? It would be like talking to a total stranger about my deepest fear.

In desperation I said, *"God, please don't let my baby die."*

I had never been so fearful of death. The thought of losing my son was too painful to even consider. But who was I to tell God what to do? After all He was a Holy God, and I felt very insignificant in the whole plan of life.

So I prayed again, *"God, you know I want my baby to live. But, if for some reason it fits into your plan to take him home, will you give me the strength to get through it?"*

No one had ever told me that God had a plan. I did not know where this thought came from, but one thing I did believe: God is a loving God and He never makes mistakes. For some inexplicable reason, I knew I could do nothing but trust at this point.

Later that morning, the night nurse who had been in the nursery came to visit. Apparently unaware of our crisis, she talked excitedly about holding and rocking our baby all night. Since she knew us personally, she was overjoyed to be the nurse on duty just hours after our son's birth.

My heart burned with anger. Fearful to even admit my feeling of intense anger toward her, I continued to carry on meaningless chatter for the few minutes of her visit. In the face of our son's intense fight for survival, I tried to control my anger and frustration.

Why, of all people, had she been on duty in the nursery that night? The doctor had said there had been a mistake, and now I was beginning to understand how. This nurse was no stranger to my family. She attended nursing school with my younger sister many years before. I remembered her boastful conversations about how many times she had lied to her superiors after faking entries on patients' charts.

All afternoon, as we waited for news, friends came to offer support. My parents came to visit. It was not a comforting time. I was still angry over my mother's attitude; it made me bitter, an emotion I felt reluctant to admit, even to myself. But it was there, and try as I would, I could not make it go away. The pediatrician stopped by four or five times with updates on our son's fight to survive. At eight o'clock that evening, he came by to say he was going home and would not return until morning unless there was a change.

We spent what seemed like endless hours waiting. I told Jimmy about my visit with the night nurse. He was furious. Trying to keep some sense of calmness and peace, I begged him to say nothing to hospital officials. I feared that any further disturbance might threaten our son's chances of survival.

Quietly, Jimmy began searching our trusty name book for an appropriate name.

"He is fighting so hard to live. He at least deserves his own name," he said.

Finally, he closed the book.

"His name will be Arlen Welborn Camak. The name Arlen means "a pledge," he said to me. In my own pain, I never asked what the pledge was, but somehow I knew Jimmy had made a pledge to God regarding our son.

Although at night my fear usually increases, Jimmy and I were determined to settle down for some needed rest. Perhaps morning would bring good news. Just then there was a knock on our door. Jumping up from the recliner, Jimmy opened the door to see our pediatrician—not the person we wanted to see. We instinctively knew the news was bad.

"I am sorry," he said, his tears rolling down his face. "I am so sorry!" Then, closing the door behind him, he disappeared down the darkened hall.

Arlen lived thirty-two hours and then was gone. Within minutes, my obstetrician arrived. He comforted us not only as my doctor but also as our friend. He knew we had never dealt with such intense grief before. After offering to call a funeral home of our choice, he advised us to make arrangements for a graveside service as soon as possible. Jimmy called his mother.

"Mother, our baby just died," he told her on the phone. "Carole has plenty of baby clothes at the house, but she would like something special for his burial. Would you please go shopping in the morning, choose an outfit, and take it to the funeral home for us?"

She didn't hesitate. "No, I certainly will not," she said. "I don't know anything about making funeral arrangements. Get someone else."

We were shocked. Hurt upon hurt. How could she be so heartless in our time of need? Then we remembered the coldness she had always displayed toward any participation with our family. Could it be that she was rejecting any connection with death or funerals? Whatever her reason, we felt that the door for help had been closed.

Who could we ask now? The memory of my mother's attitude toward this pregnancy lingered in our minds. She did not seem to be the one to turn to in our time of trouble. Then we thought of Jimmy's Aunt Claire and Uncle Herbert. Surely they would not turn us down.

When Jimmy phoned them, they both graciously agreed to do whatever we needed to help ease our time of grief. Early the next morning they went together to purchase a tiny blue outfit for a premature newborn. After making the funeral arrangements for a graveside service that afternoon, they came to my hospital room to tell me every detail they had arranged.

As painful as these details were at the time, the love from these two dear ones brought much comfort to me. It was so difficult to be unable to attend the service. Reluctantly, Jimmy left me at the hospital and went alone to the cemetery. Jimmy's mother, Opal, did attend the service, but my mother came to the hospital to stay with me. This was not my choice, but she insisted.

My mother's attempt at small talk for the hour-long visit was peppered with comments that only hurt me more deeply. She reminded me that we had three children and that was obviously enough.

"God knows you have enough to do, and that is why Arlen did not live," she said, as if she had been given inside knowledge.

My tears of grief turned to tears of bitterness. Mama expressed her own bitterness toward the nurse responsible for the nursery mistake. She urged me to talk to Jimmy about filing a suit against the hospital for their negligence. Reminding me that we had a right to at least ruin this nurse's career for what she did seemed to help my mother deal with her anger. I was never so glad to see Jimmy when he returned to my room. Alone we talked long into that evening and finally agreed that there was nothing to do but get on with life. We would take no revenge.

Early Tuesday morning my doctor dismissed me from the hospital and advised me to go home and try to relax. I promised him the same thing I had promised God in my prayer of desperation—I would stop worrying about my family and do my best to relax; but I soon learned that the power to make significant changes was not in my reach.

At the dinner table that evening, Jamey, who was eight at the time, asked when the funeral service for Arlen was scheduled.

I looked at Jimmy and he looked at me. That was the first time anyone had called our son by his name. Jamey's question cut straight to my grief. We did not realize that our children had not been told about the graveside service held on Monday afternoon.

"Jamey, we had a graveside service yesterday," I said through a steady flow of tears. He looked astonished.

"I wanted to go!" he said. "Arlen was my brother. Why didn't you tell me and let me be there with you and Daddy?"

I felt heartbroken. We had been so concerned with our own hurt that we were unaware of Jamey's pain. In our efforts to spare the children more grief, we had decided not to include them in the service; but now we understood that this was a tragic mistake. They, too, needed a time to deal with their pain. After dinner Jimmy and Jamey went to the cemetery. There Jamey was able to openly express his love and grief for his baby brother.

Grief is a natural emotion. It needs to be given opportunity to work itself out. Although everyone deals with it in his own way, we all grieve. Death, too, is a natural part of life. From my own experience, I believe that children should never be forced to participate in a funeral if they don't want to. But on the other hand, we should give them the opportunity to face reality according to their age limitations.

The dreary autumn days that followed gave me time for intense introspection. I read every article available on hyaline membrane disease. While in a barber shop days after Arlen's death, Jimmy found a current magazine with a detailed account of the death of President John F. Kennedy's son Patrick. He died as a result of a premature birth complicated by a hyaline membrane abnormality. We were not alone in our pain. Others had experienced the same loss.

I tried desperately to release the memories, but guilt permeated my thoughts. Daily I relived every detail, from the moment I discovered the pregnancy to the time of delivery.

"Was it my fault that Arlen died? Was I being punished for my attitude?"

The "if only" game became my constant pastime.

Coupling guilt with anger, I had full-blown fury on my hands. Why hadn't the nurse who held my son for my first viewing been more attentive to his breathing? I saw the problem; why didn't she? If only I had insisted Jimmy call the pediatrician, Arlen might be alive today. On and on the questions haunted me. But no answers came and no relief was in sight.

I tried to write thank-you notes to those who had been so kind during our loss, but I was frustrated and bitter. The crisp fall weather made it convenient to stay inside and try to find something to occupy my hours. With Jamey and Jody in school, I had only Lael, our three-year-old, to care for. So together we tried to find new projects to start, anything that would take my mind off our loss. Nothing helped.

Three weeks after Arlen's death, I received a phone call. It was my mother. She started off with small talk and then progressed to the pressing problem. Instinctively, I recognized her tone of voice.

"Well, I guess the people at the funeral home think I am a very poor grandmother!"

"Mama, what in the world are you talking about?" I asked.

The door of her anger had flung wide open. While her grandson had lain in his tiny casket, all day on Monday until time for the service, no one had been with him, she said, and she sounded truly hurt. Why, no one had even signed the register to show that they cared.

I was puzzled. Where did this sudden concern for Arlen come from? She did not know this child. I remembered the day my mother declared that she would never love this baby. What could she possibly be talking about, and why did it matter? I didn't have to ask.

"I have known the funeral director and his family all of my life, and they knew this was my grandson. What do you think they must be thinking about me now?" she asked angrily.

It was now obvious to me: she was not concerned for anything but what others might think of her. I asked her what brought out all this fury, and she told me that my uncle, who was also a friend of the funeral director, had stopped by the funeral home on that Monday morning before the service. The director had expressed his sympathy about the death of our baby, and knowing our family connection, then asked my uncle if he would like to view the baby before the service. He did. Later, without knowing he was going to set off fireworks with my mother, my uncle mentioned this unexpected visit. Mama was furious and decided to pass her judgment on to me the first chance she had. She was jealous!

Finally, I had had enough.

"Mama, I am sorry," I told her. "We have never gone through an experience of death before. We did not know that our baby's casket was placed in a viewing room. No one else saw him."

I tried to ease the distress of the moment. To my knowledge only Aunt Claire and Uncle Herbert had viewed the body. Because they had made the arrangements, their final approval had been necessary before the service was conducted.

Mama would not be consoled. Try as I would, she would not listen to reason. It seemed to me that she was far more interested in how this reflected on her than she was in our feelings. When I had heard more than I wanted to hear, I brought the conversation to a close.

"Mama, remember what you said when you knew there was going to be a baby?"

There was a long silence. I thought for a moment that she must have hung up the phone. Continuing, I reminded her of what she had said months ago.

"You did not want to love this baby, and you did not get the chance," I said. "So I don't want to hear anymore about it. I love you, but I have experienced all the grief from this that I can take without you adding more."

I had never stood up to my mother in such a forceful way. But something had to give. What she said had hurt me deeply. I was trying hard to put our lives in order, but every day brought more pressure. I certainly did not need to be reprimanded for something I had no control over.

As soon as I was able to drive, I made a side trip to the cemetery every day. I was looking for answers to my questions. Sitting by that little grave gave me time to talk out loud about my pain without having anyone hear. Often I would address my questions to God.

"What is life all about?" I cried aloud in desperation. "I don't understand life, and I don't understand death! Is there any purpose to any of this?"

I never once asked why this had happened to us. It would have been presumptuous on my part to truly question God, I thought. I just wanted to find some meaning and purpose to life. Even with all of my years in church, I had no true concept of death. When the weather was cold or wet, the mother instinct in me felt concern for my little son. It seems strange now that a child I had never even held was such a vital part of every waking moment. In my mind every event centered around Arlen.

The first year was the most difficult. There was the first Thanksgiving, first Christmas, first Easter, etc. The sight of a baby would bring me to tears. Not until Arlen's first birthday did I stop my daily trips to the cemetery.

One thing I was discovering: I needed more distance from my mother. Her constant reminders and questions only added stress to my already tense life. I tried to make a new life for Jimmy, our sons, and myself. Still, during this time, we never missed a church service. Soon it became apparent that the fear of losing one of my healthy children was consuming my energy, so I tightened my grip on my family. Time spent at school was the only opportunity my boys had to be out of my protective sight.

My life was miserable. Something was missing. When people around me talked about Christianity, I would refer to myself as a Christian. Obviously, I was not a heathen. Knowing that I had joined the church when I was nine, was baptized, and never missed a service seemed to build my confidence in my good, moral life. But a piece of the puzzle of my life was missing.

I began again to ask questions. Since my only contact with people revolved around church activities, church seemed the best place to begin. Beginning with our very young pastor, I asked a question I thought sure he could answer.

"What is missing in my life?" I pleaded.

His answer surprised me.

"Carole, you are so sweet, and you are just having a little trouble," he said. "You need to count your blessings and stop complaining."

So, feeling guilty for complaining, I began to count my blessings. I had a husband who loved me and three handsome, well-mannered sons. My lovely home in a very prestigious neighborhood certainly spoke well of my many material goods. Then there was my nice car, jewelry, furs, and the like. Yet, after counting all of these things, something was still lacking.

Guilt prompted me to ask the next question: "If I have all of these blessings, why am I so miserable?"

The same people told me that what I needed to do was to get more involved. That did not make sense. I attended every meeting at church. What more could I do? The solution came to me: When I was asked to bake and donate a cake for a cake sale, I should bake two. Of course, I could always arrive early for every meeting and be the last one to leave. Surely that would make me more involved. All this additional activity only made me tired. Now I was exhausted as well as miserable. The rut was getting longer and life was passing me by.

No one ever told me that God loved me. I had always heard that God loves the whole world, but I did not know that this meant God loved me personally. I viewed my place in the scheme of things as being purely by chance; I felt I was on my own to chart a path through life.

No one answered my questions by telling me that God had a wonderful plan for my life. Since God had the whole world to run, I certainly did not dare bother Him with the daily details of my life. My plan for my life included caring for my husband and my children. My plan was already in process, and I reasoned that I was not available to God for any other plan.

No one ever told me that I was a sinner in need of forgiveness. In my understanding, a sinner was someone who did not go to church. People like those drunks and bums on the street corner just a block from our church were sinners, I thought. Sin was something like murder, drunkenness, or some horrible crime that would keep a person from going to heaven. Since my church attendance was never in question, I reasoned that my few sins were insignificant. Surely when my life ended, God would weigh my good deeds in one hand and my few bad deeds in the other, and I would go right into heaven based on my overwhelming good. That was the message I heard from our church leaders.

No one ever told me that I was so miserable because my anger and bitterness were consuming my thoughts and affecting my attitudes. Like a fast-growing cancer, every area of my family life was being tainted by my hate and anger toward those whom I blamed for the death of Arlen. Fear of what might happen hindered the freedom my three sons should have enjoyed as children.

No one ever told me that Jesus died to pay for my sin or that by receiving Him I could have a new quality of life, beginning here on earth and extending into eternity.

I spent four years looking for answers. I have found the answer! It is in knowing God and enjoying Him forever. In my heart there is no bitterness. No longer do I blame the nurse or the hospital for our son's death. I know with confidence that

Arlen Wellborn Camak had a mission in this life. I believe that in his short life of only thirty-two hours he was the instrument God used to get my undivided attention. Up to that time, my family was my god, my first priority. That was wrong.

The brief life and seemingly "untimely" death of my son caused me to search for truth. I was looking for the purpose for life, and I found it in a relationship with a Holy God through Jesus Christ.

While it is true that I never held that little son, never felt his arms around my neck, never kissed his hurt fingers, or wiped away his tears, he touched my life for eternity. Every time I hug a friend, see a person set free from bondage, or comfort a broken heart, I know through experience, God does make everything beautiful in time.

Let's Consider the Lion of Barrenness

Looking for love and peace in all the wrong places led me down a troublesome path of self-destruction. Many today follow the deception of thinking material things and activities will satisfy. In fact, you would probably agree that it is easy to become a slave to the possessions we think will make us content. We can be counting all of our blessings of life but still find a destructive companion in guilt. Getting more involved will not solve the struggle, as I discovered, because additional activity often leads to exhaustion and possibly to burnout.

With all my days filled with activity, my life was barren. I received answers, but they only left me more puzzled. Prayer was only necessary in an emergency, or so I thought, and it was therefore not an option for me at the time. Occasionally, at a revival service, the evangelist would comment on the importance of reading the Bible. Without recognizing it as conviction from the Holy Spirit, I dismissed any guilt I felt with the excuse of not knowing where or how to start. Besides, I had tried that before! I found myself intimidated by some of the verses of Scripture. After all, I could not understand the King James language, so how could I possibly understand the message? If, as I had been told, I could gain entrance to heaven through my good deeds, how much was enough? I felt I had no one to turn to.

When someone would ask me if I was a Christian, I became angry, and rage was evident in my haughty answer.

"Of course I am a Christian," I would say. "I was born in America, joined the church when I was nine, and I never miss a service."

How could they ask such a ridiculous question?

Obviously, there was another answer. Contrary to popular opinion, a Christian is not just a person with perfect church attendance. The strict moral code that many live by is certainly a benefit for clean living, but it is not in itself the mark of a Christian. In fact, we can be religious and not even know Jesus Christ personally. Self-righteousness can become a prominent badge of honor. Pride can blind us to the truth. I know; I lived in that barrenness.

I believe that today God's heart is especially tender toward those who are seeking truth. I was a captive in a prison of my own making and did not know it. In Jeremiah 29:11–14 I read a wonderful promise to those held in captivity: "For I know the plans I have for you," declares the Lord, "plans to prosper you and not to harm you, plans to give you hope and a future. Then you will call upon me and come and pray to me, and I will listen to you. You will seek me and find me when you seek me with all your heart. I will be found by you," declares the Lord, "and will bring you back from captivity...."

After four years of looking for love, fulfillment, and peace in all the wrong places, I finally responded to the invitation Jesus gives, as recorded in Matthew 11:28–30. He said "Come," and I came. He offered me rest—not rest from productivity, but rest in the finished work *He* did on my behalf.

I had carried the destructive thoughts and feelings like an ox carries a yoke upon its neck. Bearing the full weight of the work load, I became weaker and weaker. After years of being shackled and burdened by anger, bitterness, and guilt, I was drawn to the truth that Jesus Christ offers. I willingly exchanged my yoke of bondage for *His* yoke of love. It is easier!

Today, my church attendance, prayer life, and Bible study are motivated by love and not by fear of meeting with someone's disapproval. Now I enjoy learning of Jesus. *He* has set me free to be all He intended me to be. At last the captivity that held me prisoner for thirty-one years is broken.

If you are searching for meaning, may I tell you God loves you and has a wonderful plan for your life. Things will never satisfy. Did you know that there is a void in your life that was designed to be filled with a personal relationship with God?

Unlike other religions, Christianity is not man reaching up to God, but God reaching down to man. He wants you to know Him personally. By inviting Jesus Christ into your heart and receiving His payment for your sin, you can be born again this very moment. Eternity is not "pie in the sky, when we die, in the sweet bye and bye." It is a quality of life that begins here on earth and will never end. It is knowing that you, a sinner, have been bought with the price of Jesus' blood, have been forgiven, cleansed and assured of a place in God's family forever.

Why look for love in all the wrong places when it can be found only at Calvary?

Chapter 7

Children Learn What They Live

A well-known poem by Dorothy Law Nolte says it best.

Children Learn What They Live

If a child lives with criticism, he learns to condemn.
If a child lives with hostility, he learns to fight
If a child lives with ridicule, he learns shyness.
If a child lives with shame, he learns guilt.
If a child lives with tolerance, he learns patience.
If a child lives with encouragement, he learns confidence.
If a child lives with praise, he learns appreciation.
If a child lives with fairness, he learns justice.
If a child lives with security, he learns faith.
If a child lives with approval, he learns acceptance.
If a child lives with love, he learns LOVE!

I recall the first time I read that poem. It opened a window into my heart. I felt the awesome responsibility of being a good role model, and it overwhelmed me.

The family is often defined as a collective body of persons who live in one house. But a family is so much more. A family is the first opportunity of influence in the development of values and personalities. From the other members of one's family, role models emerge. Values are passed on from one generation to another.

As the middle child in a family of three daughters, I do not recall my parents deliberately teaching us to mimic their behavior. It just seemed to be the natural thing to do. Life was difficult. We were coming out of the Great Depression and there were no classes, books, or seminars designed to develop parenting skills. Parents gave little thought about how children were modeling the people around them. The attitude seemed to be, "If it is good enough for my parents, it must be right for my children too."

As an adult who just moved into a new neighborhood, I was exposed to other parents and their experiences. Comparison was inevitable. As the mother of three young sons, I became concerned with the differences in their personalities. Although all three belonged to the same family, they were selectively choosing their value system based on daily exposure to different role models.

My mother had been my role model. We had similar personalities and had always enjoyed one another's company. She was my closest friend. I did not know that our relationship was actually reinforced by the fact that we shared similar insecurities and opinions. While my love for her allowed me to justify her negative attitudes and ignore her hostile actions, I had to admit that her behavior had also become my pattern for living.

Early in my childhood, I met the lion of conditional love that ruled our household. If I obeyed my mother's wishes, all went well. Being a determined child, I often had my own ideas, and I soon realized that any conflict with Mama's opinions would result in a less than desirable course of action. I learned it was best to yield to her wishes rather than express my own.

The first five years of my life, we lived on the same street with my mother's parents. There were only two houses that separated us from Gramma Phillip's house. We visited three or four times a day. It seemed to be a loving relationship for all concerned. No one questioned Mama's deep-seated loyalty to her own parents.

The relationship with my father's mother, Gramma Hammond, was different. She lived some ten miles away, across the river and in another state. In February of 1943 she died, and without any warning, life as I knew it changed. Daddy decided he would move our family into his old original home place, and the memory of the heart-wrenching goodbye between my mother and her mother is still clear in my mind. As Mama, Daddy, my two sisters, and I squeezed into the cab of the pickup truck and drove away, Gramma Phillips stood on the curb wringing her hands and sobbing softly.

I felt as though we were moving to the other side of the world. A five-year-old cannot comprehend distance. To Mama, it was like we were moving to Alaska. There would be no short walks between our houses twice a day, and since Gramma and Grampa Phillips did not own a car, they had never learned to drive. All our visits would require Mama to drive to their house. The only consolation for Mama was the telephone. She and Gramma talked for several hours every morning.

We continued to attend the same church. During the summer months, my father came home for lunch every day. As soon as he returned to work, Mama would load all of us in the family car and we would go to Gramma's house. Afternoons there were boring. I loved my grandparents, but there was no television and nothing to do. For several hours we would just swing on the front porch or rock in the hard wooden rockers. Mama seemed so content to just be with Gramma and Grampa. They would talk for a while and then just sit quietly together.

Listening to their conversation, I marveled that they were so compatible. Their priorities were extreme opposites. Usually people who have so little in common don't get along, but I sensed a bond that seemed to go beyond just their obvious love for one another. It was as if something had established a permanent attachment between my mother and her parents.

Even as a child I could see that Gramma Phillips was a meticulous housekeeper. Her furnishings were very simple but always spotless. Every Friday, without fail, she got down on her knees and hand-scrubbed all of the hardwood floors in her six-room house. You could set your watch by her schedule of mealtimes—breakfast at seven, lunch at twelve, and dinner at five. Even at my young age, I admired her sense of order.

Mama, on the other hand, was totally uninterested in housework. Although she was an excellent cook, she never planned menus, and mealtime was whenever she got around to it. When I search for a memory of housekeeping chores that brought her any joy, I picture Mama washing our clothes in her wringer washer. Summer or winter she would spend a long time out at her clothesline, carefully handling her wash. Daddy often said that if you dropped a dirty sock, Mama would catch it before it hit the floor. She could put together a load of clothes to be washed from out of nowhere. Today my family describes me the same way.

Now ironing was another story. The basket of rough, dry clothes would pile higher and higher until finally, in our teenage years, one of us would take a full Saturday to work our way down to the bottom of the basket, vowing never to let this happen again. But nothing changed.

Even with their obvious differences, I never remember hearing Gramma Phillips criticize my mother. I have often wished that some of Gramma's sense of order would have rubbed off on my mother, but for their part, they seemed to completely accept any differences between them. Unlike most mother-daughter relationships, Gramma never made suggestions to Mama about improving her life. Their relationship was my first encounter with true unconditional love.

As I look back at my relationship with my mother, I am reminded that some people are easy to love, while others present a real challenge to even get along with—Mama was both. She possessed a striking outward beauty. Even without the use of makeup, her complexion could be described as one of "peaches-and-cream." Naturally curly hair, peppered with gray, framed her face with softness. There was never a need for permanents, beauty shop appointments, or hair curlers for my mother.

Her natural beauty created envy among her friends at church. No perfume, no nail polish, and only very simple jewelry. Birthdays presented quite a problem for gift-giving. We would laugh when Mama would receive a gift from her cousin Ettie. Determined to glamorize Mama, the gift would be a pair of expensive but gaudy earrings, or a complete set of the most popular fragrance products. Ettie loved silky scarves and always tucked the latest style in the package for Mama to drape around her neck. Mama just packed them away in her cedar chest. Of course, a phone call would follow, and Ettie would ask how Mama liked her gift. Year after year, Mama would try without success to convince her cousin that the gift was nice but just not her style.

"Well, you just need to change," Ettie would say.

We all knew Mama had no intention of changing. Although she admired beautiful things, her plain-Jane taste kept her from venturing out into any daring accessories. The last thing she wanted to do was draw attention to herself.

"Don't ever waste your money on a corsage for me," she often said. "I don't like them. In fact, I would just as soon have a potted plant on my shoulder."

The only exception was every Mother's Day when she would wear one white rose pinned to her dress in honor of her deceased mother. But she always kept those simple too: never any ribbon or extra greenery attached, and certainly nothing purchased from a florist.

While she was the picture of a true Southern matron, she was also known by her church friends and family to be a highly explosive person. On numerous occasions I saw her react to a situation with extreme hostility and hurtful language. As if a nerve had been touched, her tone of voice would change in a flash, and her boldness to face opposition would overrule her usual compliant nature. It was as if she had a split personality whose evil side lay dormant until awakened. Fear of accidentally crossing my mother kept me on guard to avoid touching off an explosion.

I remember one incident that happened when my younger sister managed a convenience store, Mama went over to take her supper. As they stood talking at the front register, a tall, well-dressed man approached the counter.

"Give me all of your money and no one will get hurt," he said while pointing a shotgun directly at my sister.

Without hesitation or argument, she began filling a bag with the contents of the cash register. My mother, on the other hand, was furious. Turning toward the man and shaking a sandwich in his face, Mama spoke with determination in her voice.

"Do you want her supper too?"

He was shocked. Totally unprepared for her reaction in the face of danger, he turned in her direction and spoke in a very stern tone of voice.

"Lady, you had better shut up, or I will shoot both of you." Then he scooped up the bag of money and ran out into the darkness.

For someone who was so insecure around her peers, my mother could muster great courage when confronted with what she considered to be a threat to her space. She did not blink at the threat of danger. At that moment her fury was so intense, she threw all caution and safety to the wind.

The next day when she told me about this encounter with the robber, she seemed very pleased that she had stood up for what was right. It didn't matter to her that she had put her daughter as well as herself in danger.

"No one is going to take advantage of me again," she said in a haughty tone.

The next evening she went again to be with my sister on her job. Just before closing time, the police arrived. They asked my mother and sister if they would be willing to come to possibly identify the man they believed was the robber from the night before.

"You bet I will," Mama said angrily. "I want to look him in the face one more time and let him know he doesn't scare me!"

Nothing could have prepared my mother for the events that followed. Instead of going to identify the robber at a local jail, she and my sister were driven to a funeral home. She could look him in the face all right, but he could not hear her bold words of contempt. He was dead. While attempting another robbery earlier that evening, he had been shot to death by his intended victim.

What a difference a day makes. Tearfully the next day, Mama told me how her knees seemed to turn to jelly and her heart felt sick as she stood in that cold viewing room. Identifying the lifeless face as the one she had stood defiantly next to the evening before made her realize how close she and her daughter had come to being his victims.

Even her apparent boldness in the face of danger had been out of character for her. Normally she would never be that assertive. For instance, she always chose to stay in the background and remain totally unnoticed. Year after year she would join the PTA at our school, but she never got involved or even attended the meetings. Often I asked her why she would not participate as an active member instead of in name only. Always her reason was the same.

"I don't feel comfortable with those other mothers," she would say. "They only get involved to show off their new clothes, and I don't dress like they do."

I could never convince her to become a grade mother for my class. She would willingly prepare goodies for any class party when asked, but she refused to take a position of leadership.

This was always a disappointment to me. I loved her and wanted my friends and teachers to get to know her.

I would say, "Mama you are so pretty. I think you look better than any of the other mothers."

"Well, what are you after?" was her reply.

That hurt. However, I found comfort in knowing that she rejected everyone's compliments, not just mine. Many times I heard friends at church try to compliment her obvious beauty or natural gifts. She always responded with a sarcastic remark that often left them devastated and fearful of saying anything further.

For years I had been able to cope with our differences. Now I was a mother, attending the same church functions and struggling to establish my own priorities. How could I continue to be the devoted daughter and also be the wife and mother I wanted to be? My desire to establish my own life caused dissension in our relationship. Mama could not understand why, even though we lived only a half mile away, we could not talk for hours on the phone each morning, and what could I possibly be so busy with in the afternoon that would keep me from bringing the children to visit? After all, she had been loyal to her mother, she reminded me. She often closed our conversations with a statement that cut to the bone.

"Remember, Carole, I won't be here forever," she would say in a very pitiful tone. "You will miss me when I die."

I knew when that time came, I would miss her terribly. You cannot share every day of your life with any person and not expect a terrible void when death comes. The thought of my mother dying filled me with a sense of horror, yet at the same time, I felt she was manipulating my feelings. She made me feel guilty when I didn't spend time with her. How could I balance all my desires and meet everybody's need? I felt like a rubber band stretched to the breaking point. If I turned loose of Mama, how would I live with myself? If I turned loose of Jimmy and the children, what would become of my own family?

There was no doubt my love was being tested in a severe manner. I needed some answers, but I did not know how to explain the problem.

When Mama was hostile toward me because I tried to meet my family's needs, I wanted to fight. She felt betrayed and then heaped shame on me for not spending all of my time with her. I felt more and more guilty.

Jimmy was not a great deal of help. He was sorry that I was hurting, but he could not understand Mama's control over my life. He began to resent her interference and controlling influence on our family. Now I was caught between the two people I loved the most.

In utter desperation, I knew I needed to talk with someone. My mind raced with questions that needed answers. Why was Mama so possessive? Where did her hostility toward my husband in particular and men in general come from? Why was she like a walking time bomb, gentle as a lamb one moment and explosive the next?

The stress ate away at our relationship. Could I dare share my concerns with anyone? What would someone think of me if I expressed the guilt and frustration I felt about my mother? After all, we were always told you are to love your parents and honor them. Was I the only one who could see Mama's insecurities?

One day in the midst of my most intense dilemma, Jimmy's step-grandmother called.

Without any invitation from me, she said, "Carole, I am coming over in the morning. I will bring a hen and we will make chicken and dumplings."

I wanted to make some excuse about being too busy, but before I could say anything, she said goodbye and the conversation was over. Of all the people I knew, I felt I did not need to talk to her. After all, she had known my mother all her life and probably would not understand. Grandmother Clark, as we called her, was a very strong-willed person who spoke her mind freely, and she unknowingly intimidated me.

Knowing tomorrow had been planned with Grandmother Clark, I carefully avoided telling my mother. She knew Jimmy's step-grandmother from church, and their personalities clashed. Although Jimmy was only a step-grandson, Grandmother Clark loved him as if he were her own grandson, and she seemed to accept me as his wife.

Early the next morning, I braced myself for her visit. She arrived with all the ingredients for chicken and dumplings, known throughout the church as her specialty dish. She moved right into my kitchen and took charge. Soon I found myself enjoying our time together. Busily, she rolled the dumplings, and through the entire process she talked about how much she knew Jimmy would enjoy dinner that evening. I did not know how to prepare chicken and dumplings, so I watched her every move.

"Let's go sit and talk," she said when the kitchen was put back into order.

Her love had so filled my heart and eased my tension that I found myself blurting out a question I had never intended to share.

"Grandmother Clark, you have known my mother a long time." I said. "Do you know why she is so hostile?"

It was as if my box of pain had been unlocked. She listened as I shared my confusion and frustration. While asking questions and sharing my painful struggles, I seemed to gain a clearer picture of my situation. For the first time there was a feeling of justification for my concerns and a glimmer of hope that I might be on the verge of getting answers. Grandmother Clark was very receptive and listened intently to me. My sincere desire for help provided a backdrop for a very emotional time of sharing.

"Carole, I am going to tell you some things about your mother that you probably have never heard."

That day I learned that people often act the way they do because of locked up secrets from their past. This is not an excuse but rather an explanation. Too often we get defensive, critical, and even judgmental, without knowing the extenuating circumstances. Often there is a root cause for someone's destructive action. I am convinced that if we would take the time to listen and then understand the initial hurt, we could ease much of the tension that cripples lives today.

Lovingly, Grandmother Clark told me a story that brought tears to my eyes. As the story unfolded, I learned that when my mother was sixteen years old, she married a very gentle young man. By all appearances they were a very loving couple who knew true happiness until maybe three years or so after their marriage; at that time my mother became ill. The illness was not physical but mental. She was not hostile, but she would sit quietly most of the time, as if in a deep trance. She was depressed and couldn't carry on the most simple conversations. No one could reach into her dark pain.

Finally it was decided that my mother needed hospitalization. This was back in the 1920s, and the only facility for the treatment of mental illness was the State Mental Hospital. For convenience, it was located in the central part of the state, in Milledgeville, Georgia. Travel was limited from Augusta to Milledgeville, but the family physician was a personal friend of Gramma's, and he volunteered to drive Mama personally to the hospital to be admitted. Gramma went along to make the painful move less traumatic for her daughter.

"Carole, your mother was not even aware that she was in the world," Grandmother Clark continued. "In fact, it was as if her mind had shut down and she was suspended in time, unable to function."

A piece to the puzzle was in place. There was a lingering stigma associated with Milledgeville, because the mental hospital was located there. Most people who were admitted never came out. Many times I had heard people joke that someone would be taken to Milledgeville if they did not straighten up. Although they were unaware of Mama's experience, this tasteless joke undoubtedly cut to the very core of her fear. I sensed the pain she must have felt when she heard the laughter and frivolous references to what she knew to be her deep, dark secret.

All I had ever heard from Mama about her past was that she had been married and divorced before she met my father. Maybe twice she referred to her first husband as being very handsome and quite dashing. Nothing was ever said about why the divorce occurred or where this man was now. Her secret about her illness had never been mentioned. She had carefully guarded her past.

Puzzled by the detailed knowledge that Grandmother Clark seemed to possess, I asked her how she knew all of this to be true. It seemed everyone who knew Mama and her mother at church had been aware of the tragic circumstances surrounding her hospitalization. But, because Mama and her mother never discussed it, no one else felt any liberty to mention it.

This memory hung over her head day in and day out. While even her recollection of the event was blurred, she must have wondered who at church knew and whether they would ever use this to embarrass her. For her there was no safe haven of security to hide behind except denial.

I was now beginning to understand her feelings of inferiority. It was not stubbornness but fear that crippled her life. For instance, Mama loved music. Although she could not read musical notes, she would sit for hours at her piano and play any song she had heard. Yet, whenever she was asked to fill in for an absentee pianist for the Sunday school assembly, she refused. Anyone who ever sat beside her in church had to be aware of her beautiful alto voice, but she ignored countless pleadings to join the choir. Obviously the pain and fear of being ridiculed or shamed were the reasons for her reluctance to take any active role at church.

"Carole, there are more details you need to know," Grandmother Clark said. "Then perhaps understanding your mother's attitudes will help you deal with your frustration and hurt."

Carefully and with tender compassion, she told me of my mother's eventual return from the hospital. Her release was miraculous—most who were admitted were doomed to spend their entire life locked away in this state facility. Of course, Mama was still in need of care. At the doctor's recommendation, her husband hired a nurse to come and care for her daily needs. Strangely enough, the nurse's name was Love. After months of providing in-house care, the nurse and my mother's husband fell in love with each other.

A divorce was requested of my mother, and she could not fight. She was in no condition to handle another major setback, so the divorce was granted. As if her fairy-tale marriage had been just a dream, Mama moved home with her parents and spent several years isolated from mainstream activity. Her husband of five years moved on and married the nurse.

Now I understood why Mama felt such a dependence on her mother and father. They had been there when her world dropped out from under her. Time and circumstances convinced her that they were the only ones to be trusted. I'm sure that the overwhelming loneliness she experienced when her mother died prompted her searing statements to me about how I would miss her one day.

Often when I hear someone say "Life is not fair," I think of my mother. Life had not been fair for her. She had loved deeply, trusted completely, yet felt the injustice of mankind. No wonder she did not trust anyone. Mama's trust had been destroyed, and her defense was to refuse to allow anyone to come that close to her again.

In place of my frustration, I now had sympathy and understanding for Mama's unexplained behavior. I now sensed her intense pain. Loving thoughts of ways to be kind and even tolerant of her flooded my mind. I could hardly wait to share with her what I had been told. Now I could tell her that I loved her and that I understood where her hostility came from.

"Oh, you can't tell her that you know about her past," Grandmother Clark hastened to say. "That would devastate her. It could even push her back into a severe mental state."

"Does my daddy know," I asked?

"He knows all he wants to know," was her reply.

All he wants to know? That seemed like a strange answer. With my heart overflowing with love and acceptance for my mother, I wondered how my father could know all her pain and not be more loving toward her. It was obvious to me that Mama had longed for love, acceptance, and security from him. For some reason unknown to me at the time, he had chosen to withhold it from her.

Daddy was not an uncaring man. He made his living as an automobile mechanic, but he was also a very gifted craftsman. It amazed me that his strong, callused hands could work so meticulously to fashion wooden or metal crafts. In my mind there was nothing my father could not fix. The favorite gift for brides at our church was a custom-designed ironing board from his workshop. I still have mine. Today my granddaughters enjoy playing with the wooden doll carriage that my father made for me back in 1943. Not many toys stand that test of time.

His reputation at church was flawless. Some of the ladies of the church would bring cooking pots with broken wooden handles to covered-dish suppers, knowing that my father would gladly take the pot home, repair it, and return it the next week with a custom-made replacement handle.

Many times I watched Mama frown when the ladies raved on and on about how talented he was and how blessed Mama was to have such a handyman for a husband. She had no reply. It was like rubbing salt into an open wound. Perhaps he liked the praise he received or valued their opinions of his abilities. I never understood his motive. One thing I did know: He did not display that same willingness to repair things for Mama.

Why did he choose to live such a selfish life where his own wife was concerned? As if to keep Mama at arm's length, Daddy never shared his plans or goals with her. I knew she could have been a valuable asset to him. She was an excellent money manager. I still marvel at the way she made her small allowance for household expenses stretch to cover groceries, Christmas gifts, and all the other expenses that come with a family. Perhaps he resented her wise business head, since he did not possess the same ability. They could have been a very good pair if he would have shared with her any knowledge of his business dealings.

Mama never asked for much in the way of material wealth. She was not demanding. Every year on her birthday, the scene was the same. Daddy would give her a beautiful card with money tucked inside. The words were always the same, simply, "Love, Hammond."

"I didn't know what you needed," he would tell her. "Now you can buy what you really want."

It was sad. The one thing she wanted, she could not buy. We knew that a little of his time and personal interest would have made her much happier than the impersonal gift of money, yet he apparently never got the message.

Occasionally, at Christmas, he would purchase a gift for her. Her eyes would reflect the joy of a child. She would sit in front of the tree on Christmas Eve, find the gift with her name on it, shake the box, and pretend to guess its contents. She really did not want to know what it held; this was just her way of putting some excitement into her gift. All she desired was some participation from him.

"Go ahead and open the box if you can't wait," Daddy would say gruffly.

His attitude of refusing to participate in her childlike game would put a damper on the little bit of fun she was longing for. Many times, with a broken heart, she would stop her comments and go on to bed alone. On Christmas morning she tried to respond excitedly, but somehow the joy had been squeezed out of her heart.

For all appearances at church, we children were considered blessed to have both parents together, but the truth of the matter was that they were not together. Mama's life revolved around the three daughters, while Daddy's life revolved around himself. She made all the decisions for our well-being alone; he remained distant and refrained from any decisions pertaining to the family. It was as if he were a loner, interested only in his own life.

Conversations were very superficial. I recall times, for example, when some simple discussion would be developing, and without any warning, Daddy would rise to his feet and walk out of the room. We would look at each other and wonder what had happened. As we sat stunned by his sudden departure, Mama would ask him where he was going. She had been in the middle of a sentence. Always the explanation was the same.

He would stop, turn around, and say, "I don't want to be in any argument. You all just have it your way."

Only one time do I recall Mama having the opportunity to finish her conversation without having him leaving the room. In June of 1976 Daddy died from liver cancer. Mama, my sister, and I had been caring for him during his last month at home. As we waited for the funeral home hearse to arrive, Mama made a statement I will never forget.

"There were so many things I wanted to talk to him about," she said tearfully, "but he would never listen."

I said, "Go in that bedroom and talk to him now."

"But he is already dead," she replied. "He can't hear me."

"Then he can't walk out on you again, can he?" I said.

A smile graced her tear-stained face. For the next forty-five minutes she stood alone by his bed, held his hand, and talked about the many things she had wanted to share with him. I do not know what she talked about, but the release she gained was evident.

Since I was not there in the beginning of their marriage, I wondered which came first, her insecurity or his selfishness? Whatever the root cause, I could see that unconditional love had been absent throughout their marriage of forty-four years. My heart grieved for both of them.

Today, we are encouraged to face our frustrations, confront those who have hurt us, and basically get in touch with our inner feelings. I marvel at how far we have come. Apparently, the attitude of Mama's day was one of denial and secrecy. How sad.

Relationships cannot thrive without communication. From experience I know that whatever we refuse to deal with just gets packed in and eventually becomes a source of painful emotional infection. Like a thorn in the flesh, ignoring it will not remove it. The body's natural response to a foreign object is to react and fight it from the inside. This leads to infection, often fever, and finally expulsion. The same is true of emotional thorns. First it infects the good tissue of our lives, builds to a feverish pitch of hurt, and finally erupts in an unbelievable mess that spews on others around us.

Thanks to Grandmother Clark, I was granted understanding of my mother and was able to begin a healing process. That process continued, grew, and eventually became the foundation for a healthy relationship.

Let's Consider the Lion of Conditional Love

A visit to any nursing home will put you in touch with men and women who are lonely, isolated in prisons of pain. Not all pain is physical. More often than not pain is deeply emotional. Everyone longs to be affirmed. We desperately need to feel loved and valuable. I discovered that nursing homes in our area have invited owners of pet stores to come and bring lovable pets to visit the residents. The most hardened, unreachable person responds to the warmth of a kitten or the friskiness of a puppy.

Is it any wonder that many people today are hostile, guilt-ridden, and insecure? Due to circumstances beyond their control, they have never experienced unconditional love. Perhaps they carry deep secrets. People who fear discovery of their true feelings will instinctively keep others at a distance. When we fail to identify and confront an issue, we lock invisible prison doors that stifle relationships. Then, because of misunderstood actions, we often withhold our love. This should not be.

Love is essential for healthy relationships. We should not live in the past, excusing all of our behavior by blaming bad role models. Instead we should learn to look beyond faults and examine needs. Unconditional love does not mean we agree with every action. On the contrary, in order to grow we must make an honest effort to understand the background that has set in motion any particular personality trait.

Perhaps an overbearing parent was a poor role model. A person who fears exposure and who suffers from low self-esteem is unconsciously held captive by chains of bondage. Only when we make an effort to understand the struggles, the fear, and the pain experienced by those we love, can we reach them with kindness. Genuine care and understanding goes a long way toward healing. There are no second-class people. Every person is worthy of love, and every human being is valuable to God.

To defeat the lion of conditional love we must experience God's unconditional love. It begins in my heart and yours. The second greatest commandment that Jesus gave is found in Mark 12:31. It addresses the truth that we cannot love others unconditionally if we do not love ourselves. Healthy self-esteem is a necessary asset if we intend to love others. This is not a self-centered, arrogant love but is, instead, an honest evaluation of self-worth.

The world measures value based on external standards—how much money you make, what kind of degree you have, and what kind of house you live in. How sad. That only tells us how much money you make, what kind of degree you have, and what kind of house you live in. On the other hand, God measures our worth based on our identification with His son, Jesus Christ. In Romans 5:8–11 we read that God loved us when we were unlovely, without strength, and even His enemies—the purest example of unconditional love. Should we do less?

Let's think about the application for unconditional love. Have you ever bumped into someone at the corner grocery on, perhaps, a "bad-hair day"? Immediately the explanations begin. Embarrassment at being seen in less than favorable attire seems to be the most important topic of conversation. In truth the problem is that at that moment, you don't feel good about yourself.

Then there are the occasions when we look good in our clothes, our hair is just right, perhaps we have lost five pounds. We run into a casual acquaintance. The attitude is in sharp contrast. The conversation is bubbly and unrestrained. That is what I call "feeling good and looking good."

Sad to say, our self-worth is often a product of our own perception. Remember, ten of the twelve spies that Moses sent out to search the land returned with a negative report. "...The land we explored devours those living in it. All the people we saw there are of great size....We seemed like grasshoppers in our own eyes, and we looked the same to them" (Numbers 13:32–33). Does that sound familiar? It should. It is the foundation stone for low self-esteem.

There is good news. Once you experience the love of God, nothing can separate you from it. In Roman 8:35–39 we find a list of the many conflicts that can threaten our security. Everything that could possibly enter your life is mentioned in that list—death, life, things present and things to come, powers, height, depth, or any thing you could imagine. Yet, we are assured that nothing, absolutely nothing, can separate us from *His* unconditional love. We can be more than conquerors in Him. This goes a long way in preparing us to be an appropriate role model for others. Safety, forgiveness, and reconciliation are all available through genuine love.

Children do learn what they live. We have an awesome responsibility. What about your role models? Have you accepted without question their influence on your life? Or are you willing to re-examine your heroes? What kind of role model are you to those who are watching your responses and lifestyle habits? Will they see the clear witness of an individual who can say, "I know who I am in Christ"? If you have received love unconditionally, do not inflict conditional love in your relationships. You are loved by God; therefore, you are truly blessed. You are to share this blessing.

There is only one sinless role model for us to measure up to. Ephesians 4:15 tells us to grow up into Him—*Jesus.* Then we won't be like children tossed to and fro. We will be able to resist the tendency to be carried about by every whim or opinion. We will stumble and fall, but there is forgiveness and restoration. As part of the body of Christ, we are to help one another through unconditional love.

Remember, you are important to God, and you are valuable to those around you! Live like it!

CHAPTER 8

☙

LIFE—IS THIS ALL THERE IS?

Long before "trick or treat" became a popular celebration for Halloween, our area of Georgia celebrated the Fourth of July with "Fantastics Day." There were parades, barbecue dinners, and dress-up time for the kids. Costumes were simple and could be easily assembled by a visit to the closet. First we borrowed old, oversized dresses for the girls, and men's pants, suspenders, and shirts for the boys. Next came two large feather pillows to help fill out the adult clothes. With our pillows secured, one in front and one behind, by an old belt, we had the appearance of being "pleasingly plump."

A big wooden stick to use as a walking cane or to strike a friendly blow across someone's pillow completed the comical outfit. The only purchased part of our disguise was a "dough face." Because the temperature on the Fourth of July is extremely hot in Georgia, this mask was made of heavily starched cheese cloth. The molded cloth was rigid in appearance and ghostly white in color, with only a smidgen of rouge on the cheeks. Dressed in our makeshift disguises, we strolled through the neighborhood just to draw attention. Neighbors pretended not to recognize us. Their laughter was the only treat we expected.

To this day I don't know the reason for this custom, nor why it faded; but it was fun while it lasted. Years later I remembered the same sense of amusement when my children began trick or treating. Their costumes usually resembled some cartoon character. We didn't allow anything scary, so through the years we saw many clown faces with fixed smiles. The fun came when the children tried to talk. You could recognize their voices, but the expression on their mask covered their true feelings.

For instance, there was the occasion when Jody burst into tears after accidentally pinching his finger in the door. As he cried from the pain, the clown smile on his mask remained the same. The other children laughed. Jody thought they didn't care that he was hurting, and he got very angry.

This reminds me of how convenient it is to don a mask of pretense to hide the pain in our hearts and the tears on our faces. Like Jody, we can be smiling on the outside but crying on the inside. My lion of pretense became so convincing that I did not even realize I was denying truth. Determined to hide my pain, I unknowingly adjusted my smiling mask and tried to keep up with life. Faster and faster it moved. Little did I know that this was going to be the beginning of the end for me.

In a time of stress, I only knew to draw from the resources inside. I found my supply very limited. Fear, guilt, and worry were my constant companions, and they afforded me no comfort.

Overshadowed by the loss of our infant, whom I had never held in my arms, I felt compelled to tighten my grip on our three remaining sons. Not only was my life miserable, but inadvertently, I was making everyone else miserable too. Because Lael was a toddler, he was easy to keep in arm's reach; but I would not allow Jamey and Jody even to go to birthday parties without me. Neighborhood children played in our yard, but my children were never allowed to go to their houses. Attending a movie, going swimming, or sleeping over with friends were simply out of the question.

Jimmy was frustrated. Although I pretended to be on top of every situation, he knew that I was crumbling inside. As if to break the pattern of despair in my life, Jimmy decided we should take a family vacation. We all liked that idea. Perhaps a change, even for a few weeks, would help me get a handle on my tension.

After carefully mapping out our plans, we set off to tour colonial Williamsburg. From there we traveled on to Washington, DC, where Jamey and Jody eagerly investigated our nation's historical monuments. As a toddler, Lael was either strapped into his stroller or carried in my arms. We had fun, and finally I began to relax.

Thinking a visit with my sister and her new husband's family would be a welcome change, we journeyed to Staten Island, New York. For a small-town girl from Georgia, this was a frightening place. The subways, the Staten Island Ferry, and all the skyscrapers fascinated the boys, but I was riddled with fear. Although we were treated well by our New York hosts, I longed to go home. The struggle to hold the hands of three little boys eager to experience every new adventure exhausted me. I was never so glad to have a vacation come to an end.

During this time away from home, Jimmy made a drastic decision that would affect our lives as a family. He had been with AT&T for a little more than ten years. His part-time investments in the stock market were quite profitable and of great interest to Jimmy. He wanted to give up his regular job and branch out on his own with investments. His plan to work out of our home would provide more time with our family.

I was not so sure about his decision, but I agreed to give it a try. There were many adjustments to be made. Jimmy's flexible schedule meant he was home early in the afternoons. The boys thought it was great to have extra time to spend with their daddy. He handled all the finances, and I handled all the worrying. Over and over he asked me to trust him, but I found it very unsettling to trust in something as unstable as the stock exchange.

141

Soon my body began to react to this new stress. I am convinced that fear and worry can destroy your body like a cancer. I suffered intense pain and numbness in my arms and legs. Doctors couldn't relieve my pain. Test after test revealed no physical cause. I knew how I felt. Why couldn't they find the problem so that I could get on with life?

In exasperation, not knowing what else to do, one doctor gave me a prescription. I left his office with his words ringing in my ears.

"Carole, I don't know what is wrong with you," he said. "With your unusual symptoms, I believe you need to take four of these pills each day, and then you will be fine."

I was paying him for his expert knowledge, so I did not hesitate to do just as he said. I just wanted an answer to my immediate problem. That afternoon I took the first pill and slept for several hours. When I awoke, I was confused. I started across my bedroom feeling disoriented but stopped in the middle of the room. The consequences of my choice sank in: if I took four pills a day, who would take care of my children? I knew this was no way to live, but I had no other options—or did I?

"There has got to be a better way to find relief," I said, gripping the bottle of pills firmly in my hand. "I am going to find it if it is the last thing I do."

Later, I learned that the prescription I was given was a very strong tranquilizer. This could not have cured my problem; instead, it would only have provided temporary covering for my complex ailments. Continued use would have robbed my husband of his wife and my precious children of their mother.

There is a certain amount of safety behind a mask, especially if those around you are also wearing masks of their own making. Up to this time I had been able to hide my innermost feelings, or so I thought. Now I knew I needed outside help; but where could I turn if my own doctor did not have the solution?

As if driven by some compelling force, I asked the same questions again and again. What is missing in my life? Why am I so miserable? Still, no satisfying answers.

In retrospect I marvel that while I was afraid of my own shadow, terrified of death, and unable to cope with life, I felt confident to find answers to my major problems. I was determined to find the meaning of my life. I had a husband who loved me, three healthy sons, and a beautiful house; but surely there was more to life than this! I had not asked to be born. I wasn't here on earth just to occupy space, was I? I felt there must have been some kind of purposeful meaning to all the struggles I had endured. But where would I find someone who understood enough about life to explain it to me?

Jimmy could see the frustration consuming me. I carefully pretended to be okay, but I was unaware of the rebellion pooling up in my heart.

Some people will stay on a collision course that inevitably results in a crash. It came one evening in the form of physical pain. I'd been sleeping in the recliner while Jimmy watched the late news. Around midnight, he shook my shoulder and told me it was time to go to bed. I tried to get out of the chair. Suddenly I felt the most intense pain. My chest felt like it might explode. No pain I'd ever felt equaled its intensity. Jimmy helped me up the stairs to our bedroom. The pain became more severe. By this time I was nauseated and experiencing diarrhea. The situation was serious and Jimmy called our family doctor. He was not on call, so another doctor returned the call shortly. With no knowledge of me or my medical history, this doctor assumed I had a virus. He advised Jimmy to go to the only all-night drug store in the area, some seven miles away, to pick up several prescriptions he would call in.

Reluctant to leave me alone, Jimmy called Joyce, one of our neighbors, to come over and stay with me. Fortunately for me, she was a nurse and knew how to care for me. In what seemed like an eternity but was, in fact, only one hour, Jimmy returned with the prescribed medication.

Joyce met him at the door and said, "Carole is in critical condition. You had better call an ambulance."

By this time I was completely dehydrated, in intense pain, and hemorrhaging. This was no virus. As the ambulance attendants placed me on the stretcher and carried me down the hall, I could see into each bedroom where my children lay sleeping. I was very frightened. Thinking that I was going to die, I wondered who would take care of my children and how Jimmy could possibly manage without my protective care?

Then a new fear gripped my heart—if I should die, where would I go? I hadn't yet learned the meaning to this life; I certainly knew nothing of life after death. My experience with Arlen's death had left me with nothing but unanswered questions.

I don't remember the trip to the hospital. Here I was in the dark of the night, surrounded by a flurry of nurses and technicians. They seemed so impersonal. While inserting a needle into my arm, they began to ask very personal questions, and it was obvious to me my life was out of my control. There is something very humbling about being too weak to lift your head from the pillow. Stripped of all my familiar surroundings and at the mercy of people I did not know, I could feel my mask crumbling. I was deeply afraid.

Sometime during the early morning hours, I became aware of a surgeon who had been called in to make an evaluation. Thinking that I was unable to hear their discussion, the surgeon and the doctor on call began to discuss my case. They did not have a clue as to the cause of my pain. Finally, the surgeon spoke in hushed tones.

"I would operate, but I don't believe she would make it through the exploratory surgery."

Now that is a very sobering comment to hear when you are as weak as a kitten. They decided to wait until morning, hoping my body would stabilize on its own.

I lay perfectly still. I remembered the glucose feedings I had been given back when I was so sick with my first pregnancy. The severe nausea had stopped then, so I tried to relax enough to let the glucose work now. Jimmy sat quietly beside my bed and held my hand with such tenderness. It brought tears to my eyes. My own doctor arrived and I felt a sigh of relief.

"At last someone who knows me," I thought.

He was a sensitive, grandfatherly figure, and before I could ask any questions, he took my hand in his gentle hands and assured me that I was over the worst of it. He told me that I would be fine in no time.

"Young lady you almost died last night, and we don't even know what is wrong with you," he said lovingly. "If it is all right with you, we would like to keep you here in the hospital and run some tests to try to diagnose your problem."

"I don't mind at all," I said. I sounded like a little girl who had been miraculously rescued from a dangerous precipice.

Having stared death in the face, I agreed to anything that would help shed some light on my situation. Jimmy tried not to show his desperate concern, but I knew he was eager for me to have any tests that would disclose, once and for all, what was causing me such stressful symptoms.

For the next eleven days, I was poked, prodded, and x-rayed for each symptom I complained about. Jimmy, with the help of neighbors and friends, managed to keep the family well taken care of. It was a little disappointing to me that my family could go on without my personal, controlling touch. Now all I needed to do was concentrate on getting well.

Shortly after lunch, my doctor paid an unexpected visit. Settling down in a large, comfortable chair, he began to flip through my medical records and reported the results of the tests, one by one. Everything was normal. I did not understand.

"Carole," he said in a very serious voice, "I have some very bad news for you."

Bracing myself for the worst, I asked him to tell me how bad it was. You probably can imagine what I thought he was going to say: my condition must be a terminal illness.

"Well," he said, "we can't find anything wrong with you. We don't know what was causing your pain, and we found no source of the hemorrhaging."

"Apparently, you brought this attack on yourself. All I can tell you is that it must just be your nerves!"

I was furious. To think that I had nearly died and then endured extensive tests, and they found nothing. This made me very angry. As if to defend myself, I snapped out the only answer I knew.

"You must be wrong! I am a Christian! It can't be my nerves," I said in my most authoritative voice.

"Well, that is all well and good," he replied, "but it may surprise you to know Christians are not perfect. They get sick and sometimes they die. Stress can be deadly. You apparently have too much stress in your life."

This was not at all what I wanted to hear. How could I be so sick from stress? I refused to believe his report. I tried to explain that I did not have any stress. My husband loved me, and my children were almost perfect. What could possibly cause such life-threatening stress in my life? I tried to build a convincing case. When I saw that I was making no progress with this doctor, I wrapped up my anger and let it fly.

"If you can't find any problems, let me go home," I said defiantly. "I will get to the bottom of this if it is the last thing I do."

He smiled. "All right, I will sign the release papers for dismissal tomorrow. But this afternoon I want you to rest and relax. Don't worry about anything. And try to get a handle on your tension before you go home so you won't have to come back."

I was fuming. What a ridiculous prescription. I could hardly wait for Jimmy to come by for our afternoon visit.

Alone, with nothing to do but wait, I was glad when Nancy, the wife of Jimmy's cousin, arrived to visit. Now that I finally had someone to talk to, I ranted and raved about the lack of competence in the medical world. Nancy and I had been close friends since Jimmy and I had married; we knew each other well. With children about the same age, we were always talking about the difficulty of parenting. She had been there for me when all my other difficulties invaded my life.

"Nancy, of all people, will understand my frustration," I thought.

Shortly after she arrived, I received a phone call. It was Nancy's mother. She did not seem to want to talk with me, but immediately asked to speak to Nancy.

After just a moment of conversation, Nancy said, "I am glad you called. I will go right now and check it out."

"What is wrong?" I asked.

"Oh, it's nothing," she said hurriedly. "Mother is watching my children and is just overreacting to some little problem. I told her to call me if she needed me, so, I'd better go and see what I can do."

Thirty minutes later, Wheldon, Nancy's husband, dropped by to visit. I told him about the phone call, but he seemed uninterested. Brushing aside my concerns over Nancy's quick departure, he assured me everything would be taken care of; not to worry. He suspected that with all the children out of school for spring break, they had probably got into a simple argument.

Two hours later, Wheldon was still visiting. It was the middle of the afternoon on a work day. Why was he spending his day off at the hospital? I thought this was very strange behavior. He certainly did not seem to be in any hurry. After we'd talked about everything we could think of, Jimmy arrived. Immediately I knew something was wrong. He looked exhausted, worried, and angry.

"Jimmy, what on earth has happened?" I asked. "You look like you have seen a ghost."

"Carole," he said in his most agitated tone. "It was not Nancy's children in trouble, it was our two sons, Jamey and Jody."

Continuing with a detailed description, he told me that the phone call from Nancy's mother was the result of a phone call she had received from our maid, Emma. Emma worked for me two days a week and for Nancy two days a week. There had been an accident. Fortunately, Emma had the presence of mind to call Nancy's mother. Nancy had left my room in order to be in the emergency room in the very same hospital to meet our neighbor who was bringing Jamey in for treatment. I then learned that Wheldon's two-hour stay had not been just a friendly visit but was an arrangement by Nancy to have someone with me in case the news was bad.

Needless to say, I fell apart emotionally. Talk about nerves; I had a major case of them now. Questions flooded my mind. What kind of treatment did Jamey need? What had happened to him and why? Was he going to be all right? Where was Jody? Who had Lael?

Taking a deep breath as if to finally get his own thoughts together, Jimmy began to explain. Around noon, he had left our sons with Emma so that he could run an errand before he was to visit me at the hospital. During this time, Jamey and Jody decided to make a rocket, so they searched for something to use as an explosive. On several occasions they had observed their father taking a can of gunpowder down from the cabinet in his workshop in order to fire one of the Civil War black powder guns that he made as a hobby. From Jimmy's workshop, which was off limits to them, they had obtained some course grain black gunpowder. Jamey nailed a ten-inch metal pipe to a board, packed it with powder, and lit the bottom. The rocket was successful. It lifted off the ground, but then it exploded in the air a few feet above Jamey's head.

The thrust from the packed gunpowder sprayed Jamey's face, arms, and legs with course grain charcoal that penetrated his skin. He had second-degree burns. Jody was unhurt and had courageously put out the fire that ignited Jamey's cotton shirt and short pants. A neighbor heard the explosion, dashed over, and volunteered to take Jamey to the hospital emergency room. After Jimmy arrived in the emergency room, Jamey was treated and sent home with detailed instructions for his care.

I had heard enough. Getting out of bed, I announced in no uncertain terms, "I am going home. My family needs me!"

"Oh no, you are not!" Jimmy said forcefully. "I have all I can handle with Jamey, Jody, and Lael. You stay here, and I will check you out tomorrow as the doctor has already ordered."

My heart was broken. My son needed me, and here I was in the hospital with nothing but "bad nerves." I was of no good to anybody, I thought. Finally, I convinced Jimmy to go home and at least bring Jamey back to the hospital so I could see him for myself.

It was a long drive, but Jimmy did as I asked. The hospital prohibited children, so Jimmy parked near the curb, and I walked to an outside porch at the end of the first floor. When I saw my oldest son, I cried. He looked like a cartoon character who had just blown up a stick of dynamite. His face was black and his hair was singed. His hands, arms, and legs were burned. There were no bandages covering the injuries. He looked pitiful.

"I am sorry, Mama," he said. "I will be all right. Daddy will take care of me, and you can come home tomorrow."

Reluctantly, I said goodbye, and Jimmy helped Jamey back into the car. As they drove off, I could see my three sons in the car. I felt totally alone. Sleep did not come easily that night for me or for Jimmy.

Early the next morning Jimmy arrived at my room to find I had packed my suitcase, secured my dismissal papers, and was ready to go. Even more determined to get a handle on life, I immediately threw myself into taking care of Jamey. From the burns and trauma of the event, Jamey began to run a fever. For days he was restless and uncomfortable. We both cried a lot.

Two weeks after the accident, we visited a plastic surgeon who recommended a process called sandpapering to remove the embedded charcoal. To prepare for the operation, the doctor instructed us to soak Jamey in warm, bath water and to carefully use a soft brush to try to remove any loose particles of charcoal. It was a painful process for a young boy and his mother, but out of sheer determination, we held each other together emotionally.

It was the morning of the surgery. We waited anxiously as our son underwent the procedure. Around noon Jamey was wheeled back into his room. We were shocked to learn that only half of the procedure had been accomplished. The charcoal particles embedded in his face had to be individually and painstakingly removed. It was a long and tedious operation. A second surgery for sanding his arms and legs was scheduled for later in the week. In addition to the skin being sanded down past the second layer, there were to be fifteen to twenty small incisions scattered over his face.

Three days later, he was once again in surgery. This time he came back bandaged up like a mummy. He could not bend his elbows or his knees. He was so pitiful to look at, but such a good patient. By Friday we went home. At last we could get back to normal.

That Sunday we were all in our places in church. Jamey never complained. I did not even consider the idea of missing a church service. After all, no one was sick. Jamey was well bandaged and could be almost as comfortable at church as he was at home. He could not bend his legs because of the bandages, so he sat at the end of the pew with his legs up on the seat. I don't know who I was kidding. This was just another mask I wore, the picture of perfect attendance at all costs.

One week later, we were in church again. Jamey sat next to me. During the service, I became aware of an obnoxious odor. I wondered where it could be coming from. I never dreamed it was my son. Sandpapering affects the skin like a bad burn. Unknown to me, Jamey had developed an infection in his legs under the bandages, and the odor was coming from him.

On Monday we went in to have the bandages removed. When I realized that the horrible offensive odor was from infection, I expressed my anger toward the doctor. He, in turn, got angry. The post-operative instructions had stated that Jamey needed plenty of rest and elevation for his legs. Apparently I had failed to heed the warnings. I told the doctor that we had only gone to church.

"Lady," he told me, "don't you realize how delicate this healing process is?"

I was hurt by his anger and felt guilty for my apparent negligence. Quickly dismissing my guilt, I reasoned that this doctor obviously did not understand what it meant to be a faithful member of the church. After all, I had no way of knowing that Jamey's legs were infected. It was not my fault. The doctor was questioning my "perfect mother" image, and I felt threatened.

Everything finally healed in spite of me. Jamey still carries scars on his legs from the severe infection. He never blamed me, but somehow I could not be so forgiving. The horror of the accident coupled with the painful recovery period increased my anxiety. Instead of getting a handle on my "bad nerves," as my doctor had suggested, things seemed to be getting worse.

On a return visit to my doctor, it was clear that I was just as troubled as before. He knew I was reluctant to take the tranquilizers, so he had one more course of treatment in mind. Assuming that I might be suffering from empty-arm syndrome from the death of our baby, the doctor suggested I might consider having another baby.

"Carole," he said reluctantly, "I know you won't take tranquilizers. Maybe if you have one more baby, your problems will be solved and you'll find happiness at last."

Great idea! Why hadn't I thought of that? I loved being pregnant. Perhaps this would satisfy the emptiness I had felt since Arlen's death. It sure sounded better than tranquilizers.

I got pregnant immediately. There was no morning sickness. The boys were delighted at the prospect of a new baby in our family. Even Mama didn't resist. Perhaps she was fearful about making bold statements, after our last experience.

Traditionally, a fairy tale begins with "once upon a time" and ends with "and they all lived happily ever after," but it was becoming apparent to me that my life was not a fairy tale. As hard as I tried to clothe the characters in beauty, arrange the plot to perfection, and cover up all the villains, I had to admit that just pretending all was well did not make it so. The game of pretense is frustrating. Very much like living a lie, I was constantly on guard, keeping up good appearances while denying the wicked intrusions that were stealing my happiness.

The lion of pretense is close kin to the lion of counterfeit. It is difficult to properly identify the counterfeit when you have never seen the real thing. An official trained to spot fraudulent currency does not study the various blends of counterfeit. Instead, he studies real currency meticulously so that he can spot the forgery at first glance. I had lived a counterfeit life for so long that I wouldn't have recognized the real meaning of life even if it was sneaking up on me. And it was.

Easter came early that year. It was Palm Sunday; Jimmy had just finished teaching an adult Sunday school class when Jamey appeared at the door. His teacher was with him, and it was obvious he had been crying.

"Jamey," I said, thinking the worst, "what is wrong? Are you sick?"

With a trembling voice he said, "Mama, I want to join the church today!"

"Why today?" I asked without pausing to think. "I don't think you understand what it means to join the church."

I had responded exactly like my mother responded to me so many years before. Nothing had changed. I was being the concerned parent, but I did not have a clue about what it really means to become a Christian. History was only repeating itself, and now I was the mother.

"Mama, I know that I am a sinner and Jesus died for my sins," he told me. "I have confessed my sins and have asked Jesus to come into my heart. I am a Christian right now and I want to join the church this morning to make my decision public."

"Mama, I know Jesus has saved me!"

I was stunned. Could this be *my* son? His answer left me speechless. The phrases he spoke so confidently about—confession of sin, forgiveness, and being saved—were not familiar terms to me. In all my years of church attendance, we never talked about becoming a Christian. The only phrase that rang a bell was "joining the church." That was the step you needed to take to begin a life of good works that, hopefully, would be enough to assure you a place in heaven when you died. We certainly never talked about being a sinner and needing to receive forgiveness. No one I knew would ever be so arrogant as to say that they knew they were "saved." After all, from all I had ever heard in church, that was something you just could not know until you died. Of course, no one ever bothered to tell us that it would then be too late to correct your life.

Realizing that I could not convince Jamey to wait for a better time to join and being suddenly aware that I had no reason to try, I agreed. We walked hand in hand to church, and Jamey sat with me as usual. When the congregation stood to sing the invitational hymn, Jamey stepped out into the aisle alone. There was no hesitation. As he stood straight and tall at the front of the church beside our pastor, we were singing "Turn Your Eyes upon Jesus." I tried to continue singing, but the tears flowed freely down my face and blocked my vision. Everyone thought I was just one proud mother, but in fact, I was more confused than ever before.

"I don't have the peace that is so evident in Jamey," I thought. "Why am I the one asking all the questions, searching for meaningful answers, and my own son is experiencing a peace that I long to know?"

Today, I know there is a difference between becoming a Christian and joining a church. To become a church member can be as simple as walking down the aisle during an invitational hymn and presenting yourself as a candidate for membership. In some denominations a visit before a board of elders is required, while in others a motion to receive the new member is taken immediately from the congregation. Without any discussion or questions regarding the lifestyle or the intentions of the candidate, a vote of acceptance quickly follows. Anyone can join a church, have their name placed on the membership list, and become active in the activities of the church. The tragedy lies in the misunderstanding that church membership is equal to becoming a child of God. One can be a church member and never have his or her eternal destiny changed. A life filled with good activities can lead to frustration when Christ does not live in your heart.

Becoming a Christian is different from becoming a church member in that a Christian has a personal relationship with the risen Savior Jesus Christ. Years later I understood what Jamey was talking about, but at this point in my life, his words did not mean anything to me.

I was not prepared for the changes that would challenge me within my own home. Jamey had always been a very sensitive child. He now possessed a noticeable desire to learn and grow. I'm sad to say there was very little discussion of spiritual matters in our home. Jimmy held the office of elder in our church, and we attended every service; yet, we were ill-equipped to lead our own son in a practical understanding of God's Word.

With an interest in history, adventure, and now spiritual matters, Jamey read constantly. From time to time he checked out books from the school library that were beyond my comprehension. He tried to encourage me to read his books before he returned them. I always refused, making some excuse about being too busy. Jamey, my first born, was passing me by.

Just as a mask can hide our inadequacies, it can also shield us from truth. In the early years of theater, masks were used to give a few actors the privilege of portraying various parts. As the drama progressed, the audience thought they were watching a large cast of actors. Not until the closing of the play were the few, true identities revealed.

The curtain was coming down. In the glaring truth of Jamey's transparency, my pretense was being revealed. Unashamed of what had occurred in his heart, he was eager to talk openly to anyone who would listen. There was a childlike faith evident in his attitudes toward life. Even at his young age, he knew his own mother could benefit from his new-found faith. If only I understood contentment, maybe then I could find the meaning of life.

Let's Consider the Lion of Pretense

In Revelation 3:19 we read, "Those whom I love I rebuke and discipline. So be earnest, and repent." When I consider that knowing God in a personal relationship is the most important part of any person's life, it stands to reason that God will sometimes find it necessary to bring teaching and instruction into our lives. Class had begun for me.

I have found that God knows me better than anyone else. He tailors His work in my life's journey to get my attention in ways He knows will work best. One of our sons explains it this way—God seems to whisper to us at first, then He speaks a little louder, and then, if we don't listen, He hits us with a two-by-four. He will do whatever it takes to turn us from our self-destructive ways.

Today, I find great comfort in a God who will not let me go. As long as there is even a spark of searching within my heart, He will allow circumstances and bring people across my path. Life is not a series of coincidences, but a carefully orchestrated divine plan.

THERE CAME A LION

Hindsight is at least 20/20. My search for the meaning of life had begun shortly after Arlen's death some four years previous. God often whispered to me. Then He spoke a little louder. On occasion, I believe He used a two-by-four to get my attention. But He always did so with the greatest love. Until I became a parent, I did not understand the saying "This hurts me more than it hurts you," but today I view discipline as a necessary but painful tool useful in accomplishing the desired goal of maturity.

Only Jesus, the Lion of Truth, can reveal the pretense we hide behind. While pretending is a frustrating way to live, there is something worse: living a life of pretense and being unaware of your own sham. Being content with material wealth and having a complacent attitude toward life can blind us to the true spiritual poverty we are in. In Revelation 3:17 Jesus tells us that when no one else knows about our pretending, *He* knows.

I might ask you the same question. Are you pretending to be what you know in your heart you are not? Do you ever ask, "Is this all there is to life?"

That is the beginning. Why not allow the Holy Spirit the opportunity to identify your masks of pretense and then to remove them. With the revelation of your true identity, you are now in a position to ask Jesus to come into your heart and enable you to live life as it was meant to be.

Remember, it takes more effort to live a life of pretense and to struggle to keep a mask in place than it does to live the life for which God created you. When you allow Jesus Christ into your life, He will transform you into His likeness step by step, as you grow in the knowledge of His love (II Corinthians 3:18). It is a wonderful life when you *reflect the Son!*

CHAPTER 9

𝕺𝖒𝖒𝖔

CAUGHT IN A TIME WARP

I am an incurable romantic. Watching a good love story in a movie or on television is my idea of entertainment with a purpose. Science-fiction stories hold no appeal for me. There is something unsettling about circumstances and scenes that give you the distinct feeling that you have been displaced from one point in time to another. When our sons were growing up, they eagerly watched the tension-filled shows about people lost in space or trapped in the twilight zone. Even if you've never watched a science-fiction movie you are probably familiar with the *Twilight Zone* theme. Many people hum the tune when describing a situation that suggests weird and unexplainable details.

The main character in such a story feels totally isolated and at the mercy of some unseen force—caught in a time warp with familiar, yet somehow strange, surroundings. I know that feeling. Like the time I walked back and forth on the sidewalk outside of the Atlanta airport, desperately searching for our car, my family, or even some friendly face, but none was to be found. I discovered later that I was in the wrong parking lot, on the opposite end of the airport; but it looked exactly like the one I had parked in. Most of the shows my family watched on TV were always solved in the thirty- to sixty-minute time frame. Finding my car and my family took considerably longer.

I felt as though I had been caught in a time warp. There were the signs I remembered, the familiar entrance—even the airport staff looked familiar. Instinctively, I knew I was in the right place; but something wasn't right, and I remember feeling very much alone.

That's how I felt during my pregnancy. Even in a crowd I felt lonely, as if somehow I belonged to another time and another place. My best efforts to fit in left me feeling short of belonging. I was weary from my travels down many dead-end paths seeking happiness. I anxiously awaited the birth of our new baby, in the hope that it would make everything right for me.

Then, another bizarre encounter with fate. When I was three months pregnant, Jimmy and I went to Atlanta with our three sons to visit our friends Ralph and Kathryn for the weekend. We had just purchased a Volkswagen station wagon four days earlier, and everything seemed to be on an upward swing. On Sunday afternoon we started home. Caught in the middle of busy Atlanta traffic, we were approaching an intersection when I noticed a limousine approaching from the opposite direction. The driver sped past all the cars that were stopped at the red light. He was headed directly toward our car.

Volkswagen engines are located in the rear. The trunk area is in front, and I knew the luggage compartment would offer no protection should we collide. The collision path meant that if he hit the passenger side at the rate and course he was traveling, we would surely be killed upon impact.

"He is going to hit us!" I screamed.

Instantly, Jimmy saw the car and said in a pleading voice, *"Lord, save us!"*

In a desperate attempt to avoid the collision, Jimmy hit the brakes, which allowed the limousine to enter the intersection first. We hit it on the driver's side. The impact spun our little car around and we swirled across the intersection. The momentum threw me first to the ceiling of our small car, and then it jammed me onto the floor. Everyone had a seat belt on but me. Because of my pregnancy, I had been advised to protect the baby by not wearing one.

I felt a warm sensation on my face—blood. I had hit the top of the windshield frame and lacerated my forehead. My left wrist was broken. A quick check let us know we had all survived, and Jimmy unhooked his seat belt while he yelled for someone to call an ambulance. Lael, who was five then, had been in a sleeping bag in the very back of our car. The sudden stop caused him to hit his head on the car frame, and he was crying with pain. As we waited for the ambulance, a motorist appeared at the back of our demolished car and took Lael in his arms to calm him down. He said he was concerned Lael might have a concussion and that he shouldn't fall asleep.

After the initial shock of the accident, my first thought was, "How will I explain this wreck to Mama?"

I didn't know then why I felt as if we were to blame, but I know today that this overreaction of guilt was such a part of my mental response that it permeated every thought and event of my life. Once again, it seemed we had been at the wrong place at the right time.

We all rode together in the ambulance. It took several hours for the hospital staff to check everyone and determine our injuries. Jimmy had torn cartilage in his chest from the shoulder-harness seat belt; Jody and Jamey were shaken up but had no broken bones. I had a broken arm that had to be set, badly sprained knees and ankles, and the severe laceration on my forehead that required twenty-six stitches. Finally, we were released to go to our friends' home. Lael showed signs of a slight concussion and had to remain hospitalized for the night. Kathryn stayed with him, and Ralph took us to their home to get us settled for what became a very restless night.

The next day Lael was dismissed. Jimmy's stepfather drove from Augusta to Atlanta to bring us home and spent most of the three-hour return trip chastising Jimmy for risking his family in such a small car. I was hurt, confused, and angry. I wanted to shout, "At least we are alive!" but fear of appearing ungrateful kept me quiet.

I was in a wheelchair, unable to bend my knees or walk without assistance. I could not care for my family. At such a critical time of my pregnancy, it was a tough time of recovery. I spent the next six months trying to figure out what was going on in my life. Over and over I asked the same questions: God, what are You saying to me? What is the meaning of life? Why am I so miserable? God, am I being punished? Have I made You angry? No answers came. I felt all alone in my quest for something to hold on to.

Sometimes after spending so much time asking questions and getting no answers, a person may start making moves on his own. Jimmy often says, "Try anything, even if it is wrong; at least you are doing something." Sounds strange, but that is what we did. We sold our house and moved into an apartment. There would be plenty of time to make a decision about buying land and building a new house after our baby came. Jimmy knew I was in no frame of mind to take on any large projects. I was so apprehensive about even the smallest detail of daily living.

The move was traumatic for me, but at least my time was occupied with something other than worry. Going from a spacious house with five bedrooms to an apartment with three small ones cut my housekeeping responsibilities drastically. With wall-to-wall furniture and people, there was very little space left. Previously I had enjoyed working in my yard, but now there was no grass to mow and no flowers to pamper. Jamey, Jody, and Lael loved the swimming pool and their freedom to have new friends. Everyone was happy but me.

I felt I was caught in the twilight zone and wondered if I would ever connect with reality? Perhaps one day I would wake up and find all my difficulties had been a bad dream. There seemed to be no rhyme or reason for the circumstances that gave me such uneasiness. First there had been the death of our

son, then the struggle with my physical problems brought on by
nerves, and then the horrible accident Jamey had suffered with
the burn from the rocket experiment.

"This cannot be happening to me," I thought. "We are good
people. We try so hard."

I was afraid to think of what could possibly be just around
the corner. Would it be more trouble, or could it be a wake-up
call to peace and safety from this science-fiction drama?

At last the special day arrived. On May 22, 1968, I delivered
a healthy baby girl. I was shocked.

"Surely there must be some mistake," I thought. But here
she was—healthy, beautiful, and a girl!

Of course, we had not even considered a name for a girl. On
four occasions Jimmy's stepfather was disappointed when we
did not have a girl. Often he had said jokingly that if we had a
girl, he would choose her name. We decided now was the time.
For years we tried to win his heart, and we thought that by in-
cluding him in the process of naming our daughter, we would
build a special bond. It was a good thought, but it did not produce the changes we hoped for.

He was surprised but willing to select a name that would
please us. Our only request was that her name begin with L to
go with Lael's name. When Jimmy brought the old Camak family Bible to the hospital, we discovered that our daughter was
the first girl born into the Camak family in 105 years. No doubt
she was going to be very special. The name chosen by her grandfather was Leda Carline.

One evening while I was still in the hospital, as the pediatrician made his rounds he caught me crying. Immediately he assumed something had upset me, so he asked me about my sad-
ness; but I quickly assured him I was not sad. In fact, my tears
were tears of joy. It was difficult to express my joy—God had
blessed us with such a beautiful, healthy girl.

Then as we talked, my greatest concerns surfaced. I was consumed with a fear that I would be unable to protect my daugh-

ter from all the contamination of this society. He laughed and reminded me that if God had given us this daughter, He and He alone, knew what was ahead. Trying to relieve my unfounded tensions, he encouraged me to simply live one day at a time and not to anticipate trouble. But I could not release my worry. Everything was just too good to be true. To me that meant that the awesome responsibility to meet every need of my family was all mine.

My concerns took a distinct turn. Now I asked, *"God, why did You give me such a special little girl? I don't deserve her, and besides, I don't know how to protect her."*

That was no twilight zone. It was reality. I have discovered that people are strange: If we don't worry because things are going wrong, we worry when everything is going right.

I was convinced that I would never be lonely again. I found great joy in dressing and caring for Leda. The summer seemed to fly by, and soon our boys were back in school. But I had Leda at home, and we had fun every day. I tried to stop my desperate search for reality. Surely Leda would satisfy all the longing in my heart. But no one person could fulfill my need for love, joy, and acceptance. We needed each other, but I was placing a great burden on my small daughter that would be too heavy for her to carry.

In early October Ralph, our Atlanta friend, came to visit, and he was very enthusiastic about a trip he was going to take in November. As we listened, he explained that a group of about forty people were going on a weekend mission. They would be staying in private homes and sharing with a congregation in a church in Tabor City, North Carolina. That sounded a bit pushy to us. Jimmy and I were faithful members at our church, but we certainly never went out to other denominations.

"You are just a regular person and not a pastor," I said. "What do you have to share with people you don't even know?"

Confidently Ralph said, "We are going to share the reality of Jesus in our lives."

Then without pausing even for a moment, he continued, "Would you two like to go as spectators?"

If I had been thinking, I would have caught the word *spectator*. That is someone who sits on the side and observes, not an active participant.

Now it was my quick response that revealed my heart.

"I can't go. I have four children, and I never leave them with anyone," I said boastfully, as if that made me a better mother.

To my surprise, Jimmy replied, "I would love to go!"

This was one of those unexplained responses. I wondered why he wanted to go off for the weekend without me? He was active in leadership positions at our church, but I did not understand how he could share with a group of people he did not even know. It is interesting to me that while my four children kept me at home, Jimmy had the same four children and felt totally at ease leaving them to go out of town.

By asking us to be spectators, Ralph was saying in his own tactful way: "You don't know Jesus. Would you like to go and meet someone who does know the reality of a personal relationship with *Him*?"

I did not like this strange turn of events. Something seemed drastically out of order. Jimmy had been suffering severe pain from a back problem, and this seven-hour trip in a car would be such a drain on his weakened physical condition. But he was excited about going with his friend. After all, it would only be Friday, Saturday, and Sunday. He was confident that I would be able to manage without him for a few days.

Reluctantly, I agreed.

"Jimmy, you should go and see if you can help those poor people in North Carolina," I told him. "After all, you are an elder, and those people in that church must need help."

I was so lonely for those three days. Pushing my loneliness aside, I filled my time with preparations for a small party to celebrate Jody's tenth birthday on Saturday. Unaware that I was about to enter the true twilight zone in my life, I anxiously awaited Jimmy's return so we could get back to normal. I never dreamed that normal was gone forever. During this innocent weekend, Jimmy experienced an encounter of eternal proportions. He would never be the same, and ultimately, my life was about to be challenged to the outer limits.

In our thirteen-year marriage Jimmy and I had developed a freedom of conversation. He was truly my closest friend. Having been raised as an only child, Jimmy had not always found it easy to willingly allow me into his life to the degree of closeness that I longed for. He had finally understood that my relentless questions were not an effort to invade his privacy but were, instead, a genuine desire to share in every part of his life. So Jimmy had hardly unpacked his bags when I began my questioning.

"How was your weekend?" I asked.

"Carole, you won't believe what happened," he said joyfully.

He did not know how true his words were. No matter what he told me, I didn't believe him. I listened as he talked enthusiastically, but the more he shared, the more isolated I felt. This brief trip had introduced Jimmy to a new dimension of life that I knew nothing about. He looked the same on the outside, but his attitude was peppered with a joy and eagerness for the future that was totally foreign to me. I wondered what had happened to our closeness. How long would it be before he settled down and returned to the way he used to be?

Long into the night we talked. First he told me his impression of the man who greeted him at the door of the church and hugged him vigorously. He was a large man who weighed 275 pounds. Obviously too big to avoid. The first words from this stranger had been, "Jimmy, God loves you and so do I!"

This really put Jimmy on guard. He had never had a man tell him that he loved him before. Uncomfortable with such familiarity but drawn by curiosity, he was very attentive to this stranger's actions. Then to make matters worse, Jimmy discovered that this man worked for the Internal Revenue Service. Jimmy paid a great deal in taxes and had no use at all for IRS people. Under normal conditions that would have been sufficient cause to terminate any possible influence that might be intended. But how could he explain the gentleness, compassion, and honesty that was so evident in this man's life?

Without yet knowing the full impact of this weekend, Jimmy became a willing spectator. His first response was the decision that the people in this church must be weird people. Then he discovered that the team was composed of people from different denominations. That was confusing. One by one, men and women took turns sharing their own personal experiences with a living Jesus. While each story was different, they all had a common thread of victory connecting their lives to one another.

Test time came when Jimmy was called on to share his testimony. This was a new experience. I doubt that he and I had ever heard more than four testimonies in our lives, and they had all been from evangelists who had previously lived in the gutter of life. Jimmy said he had heard so much that weekend that he stood to his feet and tried to share something that would at least make sense to the other participants. At that moment he realized he did not have a testimony of victory through Jesus Christ. God had been introduced to him when his third-grade teacher told him the story of David and Goliath, but he knew nothing about this Jesus that others seemed so acquainted with.

Jimmy continued to share all the details of his weekend.

"Carole, I asked this big guy to help me understand the difference between him and me, and he did. Carole, I met Jesus!"

"Oh, sure you did!" I said, thinking all the time, "Doesn't he know that Jesus died nearly two thousand years ago? Boy, I'm glad I didn't waste my time going on this great weekend trip; those must have been some mighty weird people he was with."

He sensed my sarcasm.

"Carole, I have loved and served God for a long time, but I never understood the need for Jesus," he told me. "I thought that was enough, but this weekend I discovered that I am a sinner and cannot really know God except through Jesus Christ."

The only thing I picked up on was the word sinner. That was no news to me. After all, I lived with Jimmy. I could have told him that he was a sinner; and if I were called on to make a comparison, there would be no doubt that I was more faithful to church and not as big a sinner as I perceived Jimmy to be.

At this point Jimmy would have probably described this conversation as his own twilight zone. He realized that no matter what he said to me about his experience, I didn't understand. All he knew was that he now had a peace in his heart that he could not fully explain. Something had definitely changed, but not even he understood all the changes. He felt totally inadequate to share with me. That suited me just fine. I did not want any part of this fantasy outlook. It seemed too mystical to me.

Dismissing this talk about meeting Jesus, I waited patiently for our normal topics of conversation to resume. I was disappointed. Being self-employed, Jimmy could take time for himself. Instead of the usual Saturday-night cram in preparation for teaching Sunday school the next morning, I found him studying his Bible with great enjoyment day and night. I felt he was wasting time that should have been spent accomplishing something useful for our family. Many times after I had fallen asleep, Jimmy would wake me up and point to a special passage in the Bible.

"Read this, Carole," he'd say. "This explains what I am talking about."

I would read the verses and then make some sound of acknowledgment. But I did not understand the things that he was so excited about. This had to be a disappointment, but he did not give up. He found little tracts or pamphlets that explained his new beliefs. Each morning I would go into the kitchen to make coffee, and there would be a tract by the coffeepot. Then, when I went into the bathroom, one would be on the counter. As I opened the car door, leaving to run an errand, I noticed he had carefully placed another tract in full view on the car seat or on the dashboard. I never read them. Instead, I would just gather up these little pieces of paper and stack them on his desk.

I couldn't explain his behavior except to think that for some reason he had become very messy since that weekend trip. Everywhere he went he seemed to drop a piece of paper. I found it easy to blame anything I did not understand on his exposure to those weird people at that out-of-town church.

As if caught in this time warp, I again sensed something was wrong. Something had changed. All my surroundings were the same, but there was a big gulf between me and this man I loved with all my heart. He had always been my best friend and now something had come between us. No, it wasn't something: It was someone. Jesus seemed to be more important to Jimmy than I was. I have often said that if the "someone" had been another woman, I could have fought, scratched her eyes, and done whatever was necessary to get rid of her. But what do you do when the someone is Jesus?

Now Jimmy felt lonely. He wanted to share this new discovery with me, the love of his life, but he did not know how to break through my unbelief. Later, Jimmy told me that he felt so alone that he wondered if he was the only person in the area who knew Jesus. He began to question himself to determine if he was the one out on a limb, so to speak. It wasn't long before God met his need.

One day while visiting his stepfather, who was chief of police, he noticed a small Christian bookstore across the street. He went in and met Roy. He knew immediately that he had found a friend who understood what he had experienced. They talked eagerly. Jimmy's hunger to know more about spiritual things was encouraged rather than ridiculed. For the first time he realized that he had been born again. No wonder his outlook on life was brand new. That explained his burning desire to read God's Word not for argument's sake but to learn more of Jesus. Roy offered to meet with Jimmy anytime to study God's Word. Jimmy thought it was wonderful, but he still longed to share this good news with me. Without my knowing anything about it, they agreed to pray that God would do whatever it took to open my spiritual eyes to see Jesus.

I wish I could say things got better, but that did not happen. As the youngest member on the board of elders at our church, Jimmy felt compelled to share his good news with the other nine elders and our pastor. They were less than eager to hear anything different than what they knew. In fact, most of them responded with the familiar comment: "That's nice, but don't get too carried away with your experience." How sad that when we don't understand something we try to pour water on any spark of fire we don't recognize.

Jimmy became very frustrated. Although his fellowship with his new brother in Christ was developing, he felt isolated and rejected by his peers—and alienated from me. Finding comfort only from his constant study of God's Word, he was able to keep his faith alive.

It was time for a turning point. One Sunday afternoon as Jimmy rested on the sofa, he received a phone call from the chairman of the elders at our church. They were calling a special meeting at three o'clock that afternoon. They needed to decide if the group of four young people called "Freedom Riders" would be allowed to speak at our church that evening.

"What is the problem?" Jimmy asked.

The elders were faced with a troubling decision. One elder had received a call from a member of the church across the street. It seemed the Freedom Riders had visited their church that morning and had totally disrupted the service with a message of rebellion that was becoming common in the sixties. Naturally, our elders were reluctant to open the service to this strange group of two men and two women who were traveling across the United States with a questionable agenda.

Jimmy said, "Well, I will try to be there for the meeting."

When he hung up the phone, he went right back to reading the paper and made no effort to get up from the comfortable sofa. Hearing only the part of the conversation that let me know Jimmy was supposed to go to the church by three o'clock, I asked him when he was going to leave.

"I am not going," he said. "I am tired. Anyway, we go to these meetings and talk about all the problems, but no one ever does anything. So why should I waste my time?"

"Jimmy, that is not right," I said in my best motherly tone. "You said that you would try to come. That is not being truthful. You ought to go; after all, you are an elder."

"Okay," he said as he threw the newspaper on the floor, "I will go, but something is going to happen!"

Something did happen. They had the meeting, and just as Jimmy expected, no one wanted to take a stand. The men discussed the problem, and rather than face the possibility of dissension, they refused the request from the four young people. Service that evening went on without any outside interference, but something had changed in Jimmy's heart.

When Jimmy came home I could tell that he was discouraged. He loved our church. This was the only church we had ever attended, but he felt concerned for me and our children. He knew I did not understand what it meant to be born again, and it was becoming evident that I would not hear anything about it at our church. The next day Jimmy called our pastor and made an appointment to meet with him in his office. Of course, I wanted to go with him.

This was the first time I had heard Jimmy tell someone else about his new-found faith. He shared with such compassion about his genuine concern for our church. Finally, the pastor, who was much younger than Jimmy, responded.

"What is it you want me to do?"

That was what Jimmy was looking for.

"All I want is for you to preach Jesus Christ and Him crucified. He will do the rest," he said almost in a pleading voice.

"I could do better selling peanuts," the pastor said. "No one wants to hear that bloody message anymore. We need to learn how to live in our society. Social issues are what people are interested in these days."

Neither of us expected his response. Jimmy had gone into this meeting with a burdened heart, and now he knew the line had been drawn. The elders did not understand his burning desire to know Jesus as his Savior, and now the pastor had revealed where he stood.

Right there, Jimmy made a decision.

"Ted, I have no choice," Jimmy said. "I must resign from the board of elders. My family is too important to me to continue attending this church. We will be leaving to find some place where the gospel of Jesus Christ is preached and believed."

As we stood to leave the office, Jimmy said, "Ted, I pray that one day as you are studying God's Word to find a suitable text for your social gospel, you will come face to face with Jesus. Then you will know what it means to be set free."

That evening Jimmy wrote his resignation letter, and we began a new adventure. I was reluctant to leave the church that Mama and Daddy attended; they would never understand this move. But something inside seemed to be drawing me to follow my husband. Perhaps, I thought, I can find some answers to the questions I have been asking if I go to another church. But where would we go?

Church attendance was such a vital part of my life. I felt we had to find a church to join by the following Sunday. Our neighbors, Joyce and George, attended a mainline church in our neighborhood, and this seemed to be the most logical choice. Going to a different church would be traumatic for me. At least, we would know our neighbors if we attended their church.

My mother was horrified.

"Why would you possibly stop attending the church you both have been brought up in?" she asked angrily. "How could you even think of attending a different denomination?"

No one at our church had any respect for other denominations. For years I had been taught that some taught "once saved, always saved," but our hope for acceptance by God depended on our good works. We did not understand or agree with such strange beliefs, and we reasoned that their belief made it possible for them to live anyway they wanted to, believing they would go to heaven simply because they had been "saved." Even the word *saved* was purposefully eliminated from our religious vocabulary. We looked at other denominations as if they were some way-out cult. With this opposition I felt somewhat like a traitor, yet I was determined to keep our growing family together.

The first Sunday was a good experience, not at all what I had anticipated. We felt welcome and found that these people were loving people. That afternoon I pressured Jimmy, wanting him to agree with me to join that church.

Jimmy said, "No, we are going to wait awhile."

Again I wanted desperately to belong. For the first time Jimmy took a firm stand and did not want to discuss his reason. I learned later that he knew that I did not know Jesus. The whole purpose in changing churches had been to get me in a place where I could meet the risen Savior. So Jimmy refrained from joining until Jesus could reach my heart. The sermons were different. No social gospel here. I was not turned off but hungered to know even more.

At last there seemed to be light at the end of my tunnel. Because we were not members, we were not allowed to teach any classes or hold any office. That was a blessing in disguise. God provided for me the most loving Christian lady as my Sunday school teacher. She was different from anyone I had ever met. Her Bible was well worn, and she taught beautiful messages from her heart. Sunday after Sunday I sat spellbound in her class. Her love was that unconditional kind that I had witnessed in my grandmother. Occasionally she shared, through her lessons, some of her struggles and heartaches of life. She seemed to possess the peaceful heart that I could see in Jimmy. I wondered if I would ever be as free as this precious lady?

THERE CAME A LION

We had made an effort. I am so grateful today that Jimmy took that first step by attending that weekend trip in North Carolina. At least now, for the first time, I felt a bit of contentment by visiting this church. As an act of faith, which he did not understand, Jimmy became the vessel God would use to introduce me to the good news!

Do you feel suspended in your own personal "time warp"? Don't give up. Keep asking for help. Someone knows just what you need. The way out can be as simple as a willingness to take the first step. Any journey begins with one step.

Let's Consider the Lion of Loneliness

We often hear of people who adopt the lifestyle of a hermit, choosing to retire from society and live in solitude. They prefer as little contact with others as possible. There are degrees of isolation. Some can live in a family unit yet keep their thoughts, time, and involvement on a strictly isolated basis. Others withdraw completely and seek a place of seclusion, cut off from access to modern conveniences. We refer to these people as loners.

While this may be the extreme situation, others live as loners in the midst of a crowd. It is not their conscious choice, but due to various circumstances, they feel lonely and isolated from acceptable activity.

The lion of loneliness can stalk its prey even in a crowd. I know; I fell victim to its relentless pursuit. I didn't want to be lonely. I wanted only to belong. Surrounded by a loving husband, three precious sons, and the special gift of a lovely daughter, I often felt as if I was on the outside looking in. However, when Jimmy began his journey of faith with Jesus, my loneliness increased to staggering proportions. Today I know that my loneliness was self-imposed.

In Romans 14:7 we read, "For none of us lives to himself alone and none of us dies to himself alone." Like a small pebble dropped into a body of water, the ripple effect of my life and yours goes on and on. We need each other. In God's plan for humanity, we are to be aware of our need for a personal relationship with God and then live out our faith by interacting with those around us.

Approximately four hundred years before Christ, Hippocrates, the Greek physician and philosopher, introduced the theory that all human beings can be identified in four main personality or temperament groups. Each one has its area of strength and also its individual areas of weakness. No one is the perfect ideal. We must all recognize our strengths and surrender our weaknesses to a loving God who will enable us to become all we were intended to be.

I have found that the best cure for loneliness is a personal relationship with Jesus Christ. Loneliness often has its root in the struggle to live according to the outside circumstances of any given situation. Yet Jesus tells us that no matter what our circumstances, He will never leave us nor forsake us. He will not change…He is the same yesterday, today, and tomorrow (see Hebrews 13:5–9).

I believe that if you are lonely, you are the only one to blame. Jesus wants to come into your life and have continued fellowship. He is patient and never obtrusive. Like Jimmy reaching out to me, Jesus is persistent in trying to get through to us. He gives us the right to choose fellowship or to remain isolated and alone.

Is your constant companion the lion of loneliness? Today, if your hear Jesus knocking on your heart's door, why not open the door? Jesus wants to come in and live His life through you. He said, "The thief comes only to steal and kill and destroy; I have come that they may have life, and have it to the full" (John 10:10).

Remember, Jesus loves you. He knocks on your door, but the handle is on the inside. You must respond of your own free will. Believe me when I say, I have been lonely, but now I know I will never be alone again. In a crowd or by myself, Jesus walks with me!

CHAPTER 10

FREE AT LAST

And they all lived happily ever after! That was the way marriage was supposed to be. Throughout my childhood, wonderful, happy-ending stories like *Snow White* and *Cinderella* nurtured my desire to have a marriage that would surpass or at least equal their beauty. In my mind, love was the magical step to guard against any hindrances to our marital bliss. In many ways I felt like a princess. Jimmy, my Prince Charming, had rescued me and invited me to share his dreams for a lifetime. Even with the temporary setbacks we had endured as a family, I had never doubted his love for me.

Today, when things get a little tense at our house I like to remind Jimmy that he prayed to God for the right wife before he married me and got just what he asked for—*me!* So it stands to reason that he should have no complaints, right? I also tell him that I did not know to pray for him before I married him, but I have sure learned to pray a lot for him since. This always brings a chuckle.

Throughout our marriage I had grown by confronting different lions, but I know today that they were simply forerunners for the encounter just ahead of me. I was destined to meet Jesus—the Lion of the Tribe of Judah—the one lion that I could not conquer but who would Himself conquer me.

During the months following Jimmy's experience with the risen Christ, our marriage could have been described as anything but a fairy-tale marriage. Jimmy and I had been happily married for thirteen out of thirteen years, but now it seemed our fourteenth year had started off on an uncertain path. Communication was fractured. Our goals and priorities seemed totally opposite, and my codependency on Jimmy was being undermined by the intrusion of someone I could not see—Jesus.

I tried to find happiness in the new church family we had found. Jimmy filled his spare time drawing up plans and researching building materials for the house he planned to build in the country. Even while living in our cramped apartment, I found plenty of things to keep me busy with our four children. How could I feel so distant from Jimmy when he had always been my best friend? As hard as I tried, I could not understand how this change had taken place in our relationship.

Material things have never been a big part of my hopes and dreams. Growing up in a family with limited income had protected me from covetousness. I was often overwhelmed with gratitude for all I did possess, but at the same time, I was unconsciously looking to Jimmy and our children to meet my every longing. After we moved into our new country home, I became aware that our precious little girl and the abundance of activity from our growing family was not satisfying the emptiness in my heart.

Early in our marriage Grandmother Clark gave me some valuable advice.

"Carole," she said, "no matter how busy you are during the day, always reserve time in the evening to sit with Jimmy and review that day."

That proved to be good advice then. Now I pass it on to you.

At first Jimmy balked at the idea of sharing every detail of his life, but he finally realized that this met an important need in my life. We had grown so close to one another, and we enjoyed our quality times together.

One night as we talked, I revealed that I had come to the end of my patience and told him that I had a specific concern on my mind.

"Jimmy," I said, trying to muster up all the honesty and boldness I could find, "I love you. In fact, I have loved you for a long time, but I don't *like* you anymore!"

That sounded contradictory, but he did not interrupt. Instead, Jimmy just looked at me with those penetrating blue eyes and waited for me to continue the rest of my story.

I had his undivided attention, so I continued.

"You make me sick," I told him, without apology. "You've gone over the edge. Do you know you are a fanatic?"

Now he was looking a little more puzzled.

"Do you know what your problem is?" I asked.

"No, I don't," he said without any argument. "What do you think my problem is?"

"Well, obviously," I said, "you have lost touch with reality. In fact, this whole world is falling apart and you won't even help me worry!"

He laughed! At first not too loud, but enough to make me even more angry. How could he be so nonchalant, I wondered.

"Jimmy, no matter what my concern is with our children, you just respond by saying you will pray about it," I said. "Did you know that is a cop-out? God doesn't expect you to just pray; He wants you to take some action."

I said it fast and with conviction, as if I had some inside knowledge of God's mind, but in the telling, I suddenly felt totally exposed. From my lips came words I had never thought I would say to the man I loved, and now I was afraid I had hurt Jimmy's feelings. Jimmy didn't seem angry, however, he just appeared to have a tinge of joy in his eyes. That reaction was not at all what I had expected, but I was too weary to question why. Perhaps enough had been said. Jimmy had always gone out of his way to meet my needs, so I secretly hoped my honesty would produce its intended results. But nothing changed. I had made myself totally vulnerable, and Jimmy gave me a big hug. Our

THERE CAME A LION

conversation, such as it was, had ended, but I couldn't help feeling that we had resolved nothing.

We had been in our new home six weeks when we invited our friends Ralph and Kathryn down to visit. They had four daughters under the age of eleven, and we had three sons and one daughter under the age of twelve. Our two families had developed a close relationship.

Ralph often said that spending the weekend with us was like going home to Grandmother's.

"You cook such big meals, and our children are more like cousins than just friends," he said. It was true. There was always extra work, but we did enjoy one another's company.

Arranging bedtime was a major chore. That Friday night, after getting all eight children settled down to sleep, Kathryn and I were exhausted. Bedtime sounded like a good idea to us. Jimmy and Ralph, on the other hand, were deeply engrossed in conversation for a few hours of what we thought was typical guy talk.

I walked through the kitchen one more time and overheard their discussion. Normally they talked about the world economy and politics, but something was different that night. They were talking about the Bible. I listened. With a contagious enthusiasm, they were comparing events and passages of Scripture. Thinking that only pastors or those who had been to Bible college knew enough to discuss the Scriptures, I wondered where they had learned enough to discuss the Bible in such detail. Their conversation was so intriguing. I decided to make my presence known.

Pausing for a break, Ralph caught my eye.

"Carole, living the Christian life is so exciting!" he exclaimed. His face was lit up as if he actually believed it.

"You have got to be kidding," I said almost defiantly.

He was obviously shocked at my honesty.

"What do you mean, I've got to be kidding?" he asked.

That was my opening, and I jumped right in.

"I have been a Christian since I was nine years of age, and the Christian life is anything but exciting," I said.

"Oh, why don't you tell me how you really feel. I would be interested to hear your point of view."

That was all the encouragement I needed. Without any further prompting, I sat down on the sofa and began to talk. For two and a half hours, with no interruption, Ralph and Jimmy listened with a genuine interest that I had never witnessed before. For years we had engaged in various discussions over trivial subjects, but this time was different. Like a river rushing to seek its own level, I spewed a list of hurts, frustrations, and doubts I had never admitted to anyone. I couldn't stop the flow.

"To begin with, Sunday is no day of rest for me," I said unapologetically. "It really begins on Saturday when I have to polish the kids' shoes, check their dress clothes, and prepare Sunday dinner."

Ralph and Jimmy looked puzzled. They were fathers, so how in the world would they understand my attitude toward Sunday? I tried to explain.

"Sunday is exasperating. First, I get up much earlier than Jimmy and the kids. I cook breakfast, put finishing touches on dinner, dress for church, and wake the children. They usually want to sleep in, so I persist until they get out of bed. Then there is the thirty-minute drive to church. Once there, we all separate and attended different classes. Worship service is anything but a time of worship. Do you know how difficult it is to make four children sit perfectly still in church? I feel somewhat like a truant officer."

"By the time we arrive home I feel like I have done a day's work," I confided. "Of course, Jimmy can rest on the sofa while I put the Sunday meal on the table. Then after dinner, I clean the kitchen while he finishes the paper and takes a nap. With little time for me to rest, the whole routine starts again, and we return to church for the training-union meetings and evening worship."

I did not like being a Christian, but I didn't know that all my complaints were just superficial symptoms of the real underlying issues. My life was plagued by constant fear and worry. Christian life as I knew it was a labor closely connected with rules and regulations that I could not follow instead of being a labor of love. The fear of displeasing those around me and the worry of awesome responsibility were the root causes of my dissatisfaction. I was focusing on superficial frustrations instead of dealing with the major sources of irritability.

Jimmy and Ralph sat there and listened to all my complaints and fears and insecurities. When I finally finished my explanation, Ralph looked at me; his eyes were full of understanding.

"Carole, do you know why you are so miserable?" he asked.

I was stunned. It seemed ironic: Ralph was asking me the same question that I had been asking for four years. No one, as yet, had given me a satisfactory answer. While I was aware that I was miserable, I certainly did not know why.

"No!" I said. "I wish I did know. I am tired of being this way."

Without hesitation Ralph began to respond to me with a level of compassion and understanding that I had not known before.

"First," he said, "you are miserable because you are trying to live the Christian life and God never intended for you to."

"Then what is it He wants me to do?" I asked, totally exasperated.

"God wants you to give up and let Jesus live His life through you," Ralph said, as if that was the only answer that made sense.

"What am I supposed to give up?"

"Everything that bugs you," he exclaimed.

"Wow, who can I give it to?" This sounded like a magic key. I was certainly willing to give up all my frustrations, but no one I knew had offered to take them from me.

"You can give everything to Jesus," he said confidently. "He loves you and will take all your doubts, your fears, frustrations, and confusion. Carole, Jesus loves you and He wants to give you His life in exchange for yours. All you have to do is invite Him in and let Him do the rest."

The room was full of expectancy. I felt as though I was on the threshold of finding the answers I so desired. Then, a stumbling block.

"I have already asked Jesus into my heart," I said. "Remember, Ralph, I told you that I joined the church when I was nine?"

"Yes, Carole," he said patiently. "You did join the church, but I don't think you truly asked Jesus into your heart. You acted out of a fear of going to hell, but there was no obvious difference in your life. Believe me, when Jesus comes into your heart, He makes a difference."

During all this lengthy conversation, Jimmy had said very little. Later he told me that he was praying for me and for Ralph. Knowing he had discussed the same points with me earlier on many occasions, it seemed wiser to remain quiet so God could use Ralph to show me my need. What wisdom God had given him for such a delicate situation.

Finally I said, "How can I have what you two have?"

"Carole," Ralph said, as he gave a well-earned sigh of relief, "you need to pray. First, admit that you are a sinner and then ask Jesus into your heart."

Stumped again! Back and forth I argued. It was difficult for me to see myself as a sinner. After all I was a good moral person. Everyone knew how faithfully I supported our church. But Ralph would not give me any slack. He talked about sin as being the state of every human being born alienated from God, instead of being some specific deed that I might have done. By that time it was about two in the morning. I was so confused, and all the intense talk left me very weary.

Ralph realized that we had gone as far down this path of understanding as we could go, and he asked one last question.

"Carole, can you accept as much of God as you understand right now, and can you give Him as much of yourself as you understand right now?"

I understood so little about the nature of God that it was easy to accept Him without any further questions. And since I was hopelessly unable to understand myself at this point, I decided I had nothing to loose by giving God as much as I understood, so I said, "Okay, what do I do now?"

"You need to pray, and God will do the rest!" Ralph said.

I hesitated. "Well, if that is all I have to do, I will just wait until tomorrow to pray," I told him. I felt that prayer was very personal, and I had never prayed in public. Oh, who was I kidding? The truth of the matter was that I felt totally inadequate and afraid to pray in front of even my own husband and dear friend. And I called myself a Christian?

"May we pray for you?" Jimmy asked.

That seemed like a strange request. I did not mind them praying for me, but I did not understand why they needed to do so.

Before I knew what was happening, Ralph and Jimmy knelt down on the floor in front of the chairs they had been sitting in for several hours. For fear of embarrassment, I slid out of my chair and knelt in similar fashion.

Ralph began to talk to God in a way I had never heard before. There were no big lofty words. Instead, Ralph began a conversation with God as if He were right there in the room with us. His words were the same words he had been using for our entire conversation. As I listened my awe turned to disgust. Ralph was telling God everything I had told him. He echoed my frustrations, fears, and anger as if he felt obligated to reveal my deepest secrets. I was furious and felt betrayed. Why would he tell everything to God, I wondered. After all, I did not want God to know how I really felt. How foolish of me. As you can see, my concept of God was so limited that I felt I had been able to hide my life's secrets from Him all these years, when in reality, He knew all about me before I was even born.

When Ralph finally said "Amen," I was delighted. Then Jimmy began to talk to God in a most unusual and personal way. I recognized that he was paraphrasing the Lord's Prayer for me. It was beautiful. Without rehearsing any of the painful details, Jimmy simply asked God to do for me what *He* had done for him just ten months before.

"Father," he said, *"would you please set Carole free?"*

I had never heard my name called in prayer before. It was awesome, but at the same time I was puzzled. Just what was it that I needed to be freed from? But before I could argue, I sensed an overwhelming desire to pray. How could I pray in front of Jimmy and Ralph? I decided that if they could talk so openly to God without using such lofty terms, I would try it too.

"God," I said in a trembling little voice, *"I am tired. In fact, I am exhausted. I am thirty-one years old and I have had it with being a Christian."*

Almost instantaneously, words flooded my mind with a message so clear that it seemed more personal than even hearing my own name—"I know your deeds, that you are neither cold nor hot. I wish you were either one or the other! So, because you are lukewarm—neither hot nor cold—I am about to spit you out of my mouth. You say, 'I am rich; I have acquired wealth and do not need a thing.' But you do not realize that you are wretched, pitiful, poor, blind and naked" (Revelation 3:15–17).

As if I were standing in front of a life-size mirror, I felt I could see myself—the real me— the same way God could see me. All pretense was taken away. No excuses were needed. I felt an abundance of love. There was no feeling of condemnation but, instead, a sense of acceptance.

Those words that had come to my mind had contrasted a cold person and a hot person. To me a cold person was someone who did not even make any effort to do right. But I certainly was not hot. Hot would be someone on fire. Ralph and Jimmy were hot. Their enthusiasm was like a flame burning brighter and spreading into every part of their lives.

Suddenly, I saw myself as lukewarm—distasteful and repugnant. There was no denying the truth. God was not pleased with my puny efforts and obviously wanted me to be either cold or hot but definitely not lukewarm.

There was only one thing left to do. I could no longer run and hide.

"God, I surrender," I prayed. *"Please come into my heart and set me free. I want You to either make me on fire like Ralph and Jimmy, or I will quit the whole business of being a Christian and really become cold."*

Today, as I think of the simplicity of my prayer, I know that it was the only way I could make the necessary choice. It was not a deal with God, but instead a step of faith to take Him at His word. I was at the end of the road. God is not nearly so interested in the words we choose to use as He is in the attitude of our hearts.

Good News! His promise for all time is that if we hear His voice and open the door to our hearts, He will come in. That September night in 1969 Jesus came in and set me free! It had been a long day and a stressful night. Jimmy and Ralph were exuberant. There were no more questions for me to ask, and I was exhausted—rung out. I just wanted to go to bed and rest.

Early the next morning I arose to start the routine for Sunday morning. It would be more difficult this time with four adults and eight children to get ready for church. But to my amazement, I found myself singing a little familiar song as I prepared breakfast. When Ralph and Jimmy entered the kitchen, they were both smiling. Their expression seemed to say, "I know a secret and I would love to share it with you!" I wondered why they had such joy. I did not yet possess a clear understanding of the previous night and its events. We all attended church and the day went exceptionally well. I was exhausted when our company left for Atlanta late that afternoon and felt I needed some well-deserved rest.

Two weeks later, our oldest son Jamey made a startling observation.

"Mom, I don't know what has happened to you, but you are different. You are not the same mom I had before."

"Jamey, I don't know what has happened, but I *feel* different. I am going to try to find out what is going on," I said like an adventurer on a quest for truth.

Since Jimmy talked so much about finding answers in the Bible, I decided to try to find some explanation for my new behavior there. This was a new approach for me. I never read the Bible because first, I could not understand it, and second, I usually came to some passage that provoked even more fear in my heart. But that evening when the family went down to the TV room in our basement, I stayed upstairs alone. It was quiet and cozy by our fireplace.

"Where do you begin to read in the Bible when you know nothing?" I wondered.

For some reason I began to read the Gospel according to John. I did not have to read long. When I came to the third chapter of John, I read about a man named Nicodemus. He came to Jesus at night to inquire for answers to his questions.

Jesus said, "I tell you the truth, no one can see the kingdom of God unless he is born again."

All of a sudden I knew! I had been born again! No one had to tell me. The Spirit of God witnessed to my spirit that I had passed from death to life (Romans 8:14–17). I almost shouted. Quickly, I went downstairs, told the children it was bedtime, and began to share my discovery with Jimmy.

"Jimmy," I said excitedly, "I know what has happened. I know you are different! Jamey said *I* was different! We have both been born again! We are Christians the way God intended!" He could see my obvious joy and was anxious to hear what I had to say.

We talked long into that night. God had answered Jimmy's prayer to set me free.

In the days to come we spent countless hours talking to each other. We were eager to find answers to the questions that now seemed so vital. Every morning when the boys went to school, Jimmy and I would sit together for hours and read passage after passage in the Bible. There was so much that we did not understand, but the hunger to know more was increasing. Not only did I have my best friend back, but now we were closer than ever before.

Since my discovery about the new birth, I could not believe my excitement about going to church that Sunday. During the sermon, I felt God speaking directly to me. Nothing had been said for months about the fact that we had never joined this church. While singing the invitational hymn, tears began to flow down my face. I looked at Jimmy, and he was smiling that big smile that seemed to reveal a special secret that he alone knew. I wanted to walk down that aisle and join but did not want to go against Jimmy's wishes. Gripping the back of the pew in front of me, I felt a strange new tug at my heartstrings. When the service was over, we gathered our children together and walked across the parking lot to our car. We were not even out of the parking lot when I made a surprise announcement.

"Jimmy," I said, "I want to join this church next Sunday. If you don't want to join, that is all right, but I struggled all through the service today with a desire to go forward and tell the whole congregation that I know Jesus!"

"Wonderful," he said. "You, Jamey, and I can join next week."

"Why have you waited so long?" I asked.

"Carole, I did not want you to just join the church in order to belong. I wanted you to know Jesus personally. Now you do!" He said it with a sigh of relief, and I marveled again at the wisdom Jimmy seemed to have.

We decided to tell no one until we actually joined. I shall never forget the reaction of one of our friends.

"Why didn't you join two weeks ago?" she said with a tinge of condemnation. "We have been working on the nominating committee, and we could have given you both a job if you had been members. We have filled all our vacancies for teachers, and now we will have to wait until next year to use you."

Apparently Jimmy had been wise enough to wait until I met Jesus, but it was obvious that our friend and the nominating committee had been more interested in filling positions. Up to this time no one bothered to ask us where we stood with Jesus. I guess all they were looking for was a warm body to put in charge of a class. Is it any wonder we often fail to make a difference, when we use the wrong criteria to fill the classes?

My outlook on life was different. My heart overflowed with joy and wonder. There have been many times as Jimmy and I have read God's Word that I have cried unashamedly.

When Leda, who was just a toddler, would hear me cry, she would come to me with a box of Kleenex, snuggle in my lap, and say, "Mama, are they happy tears?"

"Yes, Leda, they are happy tears," I would answer.

She would give me a gentle kiss and go back to playing.

I believe that more values are caught than taught. Without setting out to teach our daughter to love God's Word, we were giving her an example of spiritual hunger that has taken root in her heart.

Within a month, I had a routine appointment with my gynecologist. He had taken care of me through six pregnancies and two surgeries, but this particular day held a major surprise and confirmation of my new-found faith.

For what seemed like a long time, Dr. "B" flipped the pages of my extensive medical chart.

"Carole, what have you done?" he asked, a surprised look on his face. "Your hemoglobin is higher than it has ever been, and you look healthier than I've ever seen you. In fact, your face looks different. You don't look like the same person."

I was thrilled. Not only did I feel better physically, but others could actually see the difference in my life. I struggled to tell Dr. "B" about what had happened. I then realized that I did not know how to explain it myself.

"Well, whatever is working, keep it up," he finally said.

I left the office determined to get a better explanation for the change in my life. For thirty-one years I had lived in fear. I was afraid of people, places, and things. Fear had robbed me of joy and productivity. That fear spilled over into my children's lives, and my family had suffered from the debilitating consequences. Now, as if through the wave of a magic wand, the fear that had kept me bound for so long was broken. Instead, I felt assured and safe. Nothing I had ever feared before could separate me from this security that brought such peace.

For the first time, I reacted calmly to situations where circumstances were out of my control. My responses to problems began to sound like Jimmy's.

"We will pray about it," was my new answer to life's circumstances, because now I was no longer alone. The awareness that someone greater than I was in control released me from the worry that had consumed my plans and thoughts for so long. This freedom was too wonderful to explain.

My first test of faith came one month later when Ralph made a surprise visit to our home. He told us that he was going to High Point, North Carolina, for another weekend Lay Witness Mission. Then to my surprise he asked if we would like to go along as part of the witnessing team.

Jimmy did not have time to answer before I said, "Yes, we would love to go."

The shock on Jimmy's face was equaled only by the surprise in my own heart. Did I say yes? I could not believe my own response.

"Carole what will we do with the children?" Jimmy asked.

"I don't know," I said, "but I want to go, and I know that God will provide someone to take care of them." I heard a confidence in my voice that was totally foreign to my former pattern of behavior.

Two days later, I shared this opportunity with our friends from whom we had purchased our land. In the three years since we had come to Aunt Billie and Uncle B B, as we affectionately called them, they had become like grandparents to our children. With only one son of their own, they adopted our children as their own grandchildren and loved them with an unconditional love that our own parents had never given.

Aunt Billie listened to our plans with interest, then asked me a surprising question.

"Carole, can we come over and keep the children for the weekend?"

Talk about an answer out of the blue. I had felt certain that God would provide, but I was still surprised when the answer came voluntarily.

"Yes, you certainly can," I said.

It was three weeks before the mission trip. The preparation material we received encouraged us to read the Gospel of John again and again. I did as instructed, but I began to feel unsure of my ability. Jimmy finally told me to simply go and trust God to tell me what to say. It sounded too simple and frightening, but I seemed to have no other choice.

At last, the time had come. As Jimmy drove the seven-hour trip, I read through the Scriptures in a last-minute effort to be equipped to answer possible questions. At times I even questioned the wisdom of my eagerness to be a part of a team effort in a different church. Arriving at the small church was the beginning of the most challenging weekend I had ever spent. It was the first time that I had been away from my children, but remarkably, I was so calm it almost frightened me.

There was a strange security in meeting these new people. It was as if my desire to share my new freedom was greater than my fear of the strangers. Before the first session was over, I felt as if we were among friends.

The typical format for the weekend included separate luncheons for the men and women on Saturday. For the first time I would be separated from Jimmy, and I have to admit that panic swept in momentarily. Then I reassured myself that I would be with my new friends and that I would survive.

This was a unique Lay Witness Mission. There were fifteen missions being held simultaneously in High Point that weekend, and the ladies luncheon was well attended. There were 840 ladies from 15 teams and various churches.

At the beginning of the meeting, the presiding lady announced that there would be three ladies chosen during the luncheon to tell what Jesus meant to them personally. Having spent thirty-one years of my life afraid to speak in my own church, I was shocked at my own response. Sitting up straight in my chair, I prayed silently, *"God, please let one of the three be me."*

As I waited I looked around the room. Neither Jimmy nor my mother was with me, yet I felt perfectly comfortable with the seven ladies at my table, ladies I had never known until just the night before. For the first time in my life, I was in another city away from my own children, without my husband or mother, and yes, I was not worrying. I had seriously asked God to let me share before 840 ladies. Something had happened in my life, and I was on the threshold of a new adventure that would never end.

You have undoubtedly heard that before a person drowns, his life is said to flash in front of him. Well, I certainly was not drowning, but for a brief moment, I saw my life. At last I was free!

No, I was not one of the three called to share that day, but that was not the point. I had been willing and that was enough. God had shown me that He loved me, knew where I was, and nothing would ever be the same again. With this understanding, I was overcome with love that was indescribable but real. The "new birth" was just that—a fresh new opportunity to be all God had intended me to be. Old things, such as worry, fear, and feelings of inferiority, had given way to obedience, faith, and unconditional love. I was a new creature in Christ.

Let's Consider the Lion of Freedom

Fear and faith are similar to oil and water. They cannot mix. The fear of life, death, and everything in between had plagued my life and was my master. Freedom seemed like a concept—reality for someone else, not me. But true freedom is the opposite of bondage, and I did not comprehend the bondage that controlled my thoughts, emotions, and actions until I was introduced to the greatest gift of all—the love of God as expressed in Jesus Christ. I was set free!

Revelation 3:17 describes a life apart from Christ as one that is wretched, pitiful, poor, blind, and naked. These are conditions not of our physical nature but rather our spiritual state. How can we be found if we are unaware that we are lost? Only until we understand our true condition do we seek a better way.

Being wretched means to be poor in quality or to be unsatisfactory. That is a picture of us outside of a relationship with Jesus—totally lost! Never measuring up to the best we can be. Or worse yet, falling short. Like a sharpshooter who misses the mark he intended to hit, whether by an inch or by a mile, he's really missed it altogether.

To be pitiful (or miserable) means to feel very unhappy and unpleasant. Because things don't satisfy, we can have everything we desire and still be miserable. While looking for that one person, place, or thing that will fill the emptiness, we overlook our blessings and focus on our losses. A miserable person is not only unhappy with his own lot but is often jealous of another's freedom.

Poverty can best be described as a condition of lack. No one desires poverty, but Revelation describes a person without Jesus as very poor indeed. Perhaps we reach the lowest level of spiritual poverty when we try to live life according to our own desires and never understand the purpose of life from God's view. How sad to live and die and never know the meaning of life.

Of all the physical losses a person can experience, I think blindness would be extremely difficult. To never see a sunset, a baby's smile, or a rainbow would certainly be a great loss. Yet God's Word equates blindness in spiritual matters to the greatest handicap of all. To go through life unable to understand or discern God's love, creation, and plan of salvation would permanently handicap an individual for time and eternity.

Finally, to be naked means having an absence of suitable clothing. Trying to cover our own wickedness and sin and being unaware that God can see right through our "fig leaves," so to speak, is foolishness. To be deceived into believing that we could earn or somehow purchase God's approval, as in Adam and Eve's situation, is the height of self-righteousness.

Only *the Lion of the Tribe of Judah—Jesus* —can open our eyes to behold God's love, open our hearts to receive His provision, and open our lives to walk in the freedom that makes life worth living.

Are you like the descendants of Abraham in John, chapter eight, unaware that you are in bondage to the sins of fear, worry, or feelings of inferiority? Ask God to show you how He sees you, *and He will!*

Jesus said, "If you hold to my teaching, you are really my disciples. Then you will know the truth, and the truth will set you free. So if the Son sets you free, you will be free indeed" (John 8:31–32, 36).

I know what it means to be lost, and now I know how to be *free at last!*

CHAPTER 11

SOMETHING BEAUTIFUL

When I was a little girl, finances were tight. My father was an excellent automobile mechanic, but the pay wasn't very good. Living on a small farm meant we always had plenty of food—vegetables from our garden, an abundance of milk and farm-fresh eggs, as well as freshly butchered meat from our stock. I was not impressed with our food; instead, I envied my friend who lived in the city. Her mother had to go every morning to the corner grocery store to purchase her food for that evening's dinner, and it sounded like more fun than going to the garden or the chicken house. Not until I grew up did I come to appreciate homegrown vegetables.

Most of our clothes were hand-me-downs from friends. They were good quality but were often several seasons behind in style. One day a friend gave my mother a large box of clothes. Eagerly my sisters and I sorted through the unexpected treasure, and to my delight, I found a beautiful, pastel pink, wool sweater that fit me perfectly. It was so stylish. I slipped the sweater over my head, but somewhere between its last owner and me, hungry moths had left their mark. There were small holes scattered over the bodice. I was so sad, I couldn't help crying. At last I had a wool sweater of my own, but it was destined for the rag bag.

Mama saw my tears and held me close.

"Carole, don't worry; we will think of something," she said. I wondered how she would salvage this once lovely garment. Trying to forget my loss, I hurriedly looked through the other clothes, but nothing caught my eye like that sweater. Several days later, Mama told me she had a surprise. Carefully, she placed a bag in my open hands and waited for me to retrieve its contents.

"It is beautiful," I exclaimed as I held up the once ugly sweater. "Mama how did you make it so lovely?"

Anxious to share her own joy, she told me that she had asked my father's elderly aunt for help. Aunt Lucy had taken the moth-eaten sweater, and with a great deal of love, had embroidered small bunches of dainty flowers over the moth holes.

I couldn't believe it! The once rejected sweater was now uniquely designed with exquisite beauty. Not only did I have an up-to-date sweater, it was one of a kind. I felt so special. Of course, that sweater saw many years of use and left a vivid picture in my mind that even today gives me encouragement when I face rejection and disappointment.

In the hands of the Master Weaver—just like my sweater—something beautiful was being made from the holes and tears of my life. Now, at the age of thirty-one, I felt like a prisoner who had been given unexpected and undeserved liberty. It was as if I had been given a key that opened a bountiful treasure chest of blessings. The new experiences of joy, peace, forgiveness, and most of all, unconditional love made me eager to share with anyone who would listen.

My first target would be Mama. I say target because in my zeal, I literally invaded her space and proceeded to diagnose her problem. No one understood her better than I. For years we had consoled each other in our fears, fed our mutual worries, and huddled behind imaginary walls of inferiority. I understood first-hand the emptiness that fear, distrust, and worry had created in my life. In my zeal to share my new discoveries about life, I immediately wanted the same freedom for Mama. Wouldn't everyone in bondage want freedom?

"Mama, I have found Jesus and He has set me free!" I told her boldly one day.

Our lives were so entwined that she could not deny the obvious differences in my life. Like a butterfly set free from a tight cocoon, I had shaken off the shackles of fear. Instead of my usual worried outlook on everyday tasks and future decisions, there was a distinct attitude of optimism. Blinded by my joy, I was not prepared for her reaction to my transformation. Instead of responding with acceptance, she became the ferocious lion of rejection.

Several years later, I heard it said that perhaps new Christians should be locked up for about six months so they wouldn't leave a trail of destruction in their uninformed zeal to share the good news. I certainly would have been a good candidate for a little time of educational confinement instead of the instant evangelism path I was pursuing. My zeal greatly exceeded my knowledge.

In my burden to help my mother find freedom from her bondage, I seized every opportunity to tell her what I was learning. Instead of drawing her to Jesus, it pushed her away. I longed for her to accept Jesus, but instead found a vicious spirit of hostility. Mama could not understand my explanations and felt threatened by the obvious changes in my personality. Undoubtedly, my new freedom was causing a separation between us instead of a bonding. Looking back, I can see that her responses were similar to my responses to Jimmy, so why didn't I recognize them sooner? I was not nearly as patient with Mama as Jimmy had been with me.

For instance, once while I tried to explain that I had *just* become a Christian, she responded with a harsh condemnation that revealed the depth of our communication gap.

"Well, I am sorry I wasted all those years taking you to church," she said sarcastically.

That was not what I meant to imply. I was not blaming her for wasted time or the misunderstandings that I had held about salvation. In her mind she knew she had been faithful to continue the example taught by her mother—perfect attendance, legalistic attitudes, and distrust of anything different. Now here I was, her child, questioning her nurturing skills and expressing doubts about her own salvation. By now she felt threatened and angry.

But for the first time, I understood both sides. While I could see the frustration in Mama's life and knew the joy she was missing, I also knew what it meant to be forgiven and to be loved unconditionally. I was becoming aware that God had a plan for my life, and this truth was too good to keep to myself. Why shouldn't Mama know this joy too?

Salvation is not a "works" program. Instead, it is a free gift from God. It is not something that we earn by having perfect attendance, being morally good, or refraining from certain acts of behavior. It is a condition of being a sinner accepted by God through the death of Jesus Christ on Calvary. It is God's plan for all who will receive this provision. We can be saved from the penalty of our sin, saved from the power of sinning daily, and we will one day be saved from the presence of sin. This is good news that everyone should hear, so I couldn't give up.

Following the pattern my mother developed from her mother, I began every day with a lengthy phone call to Mama. I knew better than to miss a call each day. Yet, every phone conversation turned into a struggle to explain my point of view and overcome her obstinate rejection. On the occasions I asked her to forgive me for my pushy attitude, we would try to find some common ground to talk; but I was changing, and the friction in our relationship only increased.

Less than one month after I met Jesus, a new door of opportunity opened. Several ladies in my church approached me with an intriguing offer to meet each week with them to explain what I was learning. What a thrill. It would not be a Bible study, as such, but rather a sharing time. It seemed they had observed the changes in my life and were very interested in knowing more. Of course, I agreed. How could I even think of turning down an opportunity to share my joy with people who seemed hungry to hear.

Talk about evangelism. This is the way I believe it is supposed to be. In Psalm 40 God says He hears our cries, delivers us from the pit, sets our feet upon a new path, and establishes our purpose. He gives us a new song. The key is that, according to this passage, many shall *see* the new song, fear, and trust in the Lord. Normally, we think of *hearing* a new song, but God says it is more important for others to *see* the difference for themselves so they will be willing to listen to our words. All my life, I had heard the phrase "Actions speak louder than words," and now I was seeing this truth played out in my life. My friends seemed to desire what I had even as my mother rejected anything that seemingly separated the two of us.

So began the challenging opportunity to study God's Word with the express purpose of sharing my growth with others who sensed a need in their own lives. It proved to be a stimulating task, and for the first time in my life, I was facing a big responsibility. I did not want to mislead anyone, so I began to carefully search the Scriptures. Together our group of ladies grew, and God opened our hearts to His Word.

You cannot study God's Word without opening a treasure of love, instruction, hope, and enlightenment; but what you do with knowledge is up to you. Receive it and be changed, or reject it and stay where you are.

Growth comes only when we are willing to grow. The more I learned, the better equipped I became. My desire to share with Mama increased. Within the year I was scheduled for major surgery.

For the ten days I was hospitalized, Mama came to visit every evening, and I prayed over and over, *"Father, please let me show Mama your love, and please open her heart to hear the truth that can set her free."*

Before my surgery I placed small inspirational books around my hospital room in case Mama had free time to read while I rested. She read them, and as soon as I was awake enough to talk, she began to ask questions. It was glorious. God was answering my prayer, and I could hardly contain my joy. I was a little wiser, trying to wait patiently on His timing. The night before my dismissal from the hospital, Mama seemed to be on the verge of surrender to a Heavenly Father who had been wooing her into His wonderful family. We shared openly, but I did not push her for a decision. She left the hospital just before midnight.

The excitement of Mama being so close to becoming a Christian kept me awake most of the night. Early the next morning Jimmy arrived to take me home. Mama was due to come over later that evening after I'd settled in at home, and I could hardly wait to continue our talk. That day she neither called nor came to visit. When I called her later that evening, she sounded very distant, as if a wall had been erected and our sweet reunion was over.

Two weeks went by. She did not visit as she had promised, although I phoned her several times. Finally, she volunteered some heartbreaking news. On the day I was dismissed from the hospital, she shared her feelings with my father. Carefully, she explained to him that she had talked with me and now believed that she needed to accept Jesus Christ as her Savior.

"Don't believe anything Carole tells you about being a Christian," Daddy told her. "She is confused and mixed up. You are fine just like you are."

Thoroughly confused, Mama chose to deny her feelings and to distance herself to protect her from any further encounters with me or my beliefs. I felt very sad. She had been so close to receiving her own personal freedom in Christ and was now walking away from the opportunity, once again angry with me. From

then on our conversations became more tense and argumenta-
tive, and Mama and Daddy even avoided our family. Our children began to sense this deliberate rejection from their grandparents.

I missed the closeness we had enjoyed before I met Jesus,
but because of my new-found faith, any fellowship with Mama
and Daddy was now strained. I felt like a stranger instead of
their daughter. I responded in a way I knew they could not control—with my love and prayers—but there was a void in my
life. As I was to soon discover, however, God always meets the
need if we will trust Him.

Our move to another church opened new doors, and the
arrival of Christian Women's Club, a division of Stonecroft Min-
istries in Kansas City, Missouri, would play a major role in my
spiritual growth. Until then I had never heard of such a group
but was invited to the first organizational luncheon and found it
wonderful. The two representatives from Stonecroft busily arranged get-acquainted coffees and prayer times. They planned
to select a board of volunteers to fill the positions necessary to
establish a monthly Christian Women's Club luncheon. The
outreach was interdenominational and evangelistic—just what
I was looking for.

Soon I met many ladies who shared the same love of Christ
that Jimmy and I had. As the first board was established, I was
asked to serve as prayer advisor, and I could not have chosen a
better position of service myself. Each month I had the joy of
leading the prayer meditations for the executive board and the
specific prayer times for the monthly prayer coffees. The opportunity to work with the other advisors and the chairman gave
me confidence and developed in me a new sense of security with
strangers. My mother refused to go to any of the meetings, and
although I was disappointed, I continued to pray for a break-
through in communication. Today, more than twenty-five years
later, I continue to travel and speak to Christian Women's Clubs
along the East Coast.

God knew the desire of my heart was for the salvation of my parents. Though they deliberately kept us at arm's length, Jimmy and I did all we could to express our love. In the spring of 1973 Daddy became very ill and was admitted to a hospital where he underwent extensive testing for five weeks. Finally, after exploratory surgery, he was diagnosed with a mass of malignant tumors in his liver. No treatment was recommended, and the doctors advised us to take him home to let him die. With only a possible week or two to live, we tried to make him comfortable. Weeks stretched into months and Daddy gained strength. I offered to help, but Mama treated me like a total stranger instead of her daughter. "Thanks, but no thanks!" was her response.

Though rejected by my parents, I felt my love for them grow even stronger with the pending completion of Daddy's life. Six weeks later, Daddy went to the doctor. Tests were made and the news was good! No sign of cancer. Everyone was overjoyed, except Daddy. He dismissed our concern and denied that he had ever had cancer.

Jimmy and I believed then and now that God answered many prayers by healing my father to give him more time to repent. But Daddy brushed away attempts to discuss salvation. The only response we ever received from Daddy was a story he told about some man who had tried to witness to my grandfather some thirty-five years earlier. Daddy still bore a grudge toward that man who seemed to question my grandfather's good name by suggesting that he might need to be "saved." Daddy believed that his father was a good, moral man and did not need any religion. Although Daddy was himself active at his church, he never talked of personal salvation. Nothing we could say would change his mind. We just kept praying.

Mama, on the other hand, was showing signs of interest again. She cautiously inquired from time to time about my opinions regarding certain key questions, but she always remained apathetic about making a commitment. But something about Daddy's illness and his subsequent denial of a need for salvation was apparently undermining her level of rejection.

After a very difficult year of coping with Daddy's recovery, Mama entered the hospital for major surgery. Of course, cancer was a primary concern, but our fears were put to rest when no cancer was found. Still, she seemed very restless. Recovery did not come as quickly as we had anticipated, and she was quite content to remain in the hospital. Life was in an upheaval at her house. One of my sisters was going through a separation from her husband of twenty-one years, and the other one was involved in a personally destructive lifestyle. Mama obviously enjoyed a sense of security by being the patient in the hospital instead of the care giver at home.

Mama did not want to be left alone in the hospital, so we took turns staying with her. To avoid any friction from my sisters, I chose the night shift. Mama slept through the night, so I would snuggle up in a comfortable chair, drink coffee, and listen to cassette tapes I received from an Atlanta church.

I left my tapes and tape player in Mama's room, and one day my younger sister told me that she had listened to my tapes and wanted to know more about them. I was surprised at her interest but delighted to have the opportunity to talk with her about spiritual things. She seemed genuinely interested and expressed a desire to make a trip to the Atlanta church with my family. After all the months I had been trying to share with Mama, an occasion to share with this sister had never been clearer.

Together, my sister and I made plans to go to Atlanta one Sunday, just as soon as Mama was dismissed from the hospital. Mama overheard our conversation and insisted we go the very next Sunday without her. After she repeatedly assured us that she would be all right alone in the hospital for the day, we agreed.

The trip turned out to be better than I had anticipated. Both of my sisters were to meet us at the church instead of traveling along with us. To my delight they arrived at church that morning accompanied by two of our first cousins. I could hardly contain my joy. Like a dream come true, four people who were my close family would be joining us in a worship service.

The service was wonderful and the music inspiring. All of our guests were visibly impressed. Afterward, we stood around and talked for more than an hour. After hugs and goodbyes, we started home. Our trip home was exciting. Jimmy and I shared with our children the amazing way God had brought my two sisters and these two cousins together to hear the gospel message at one time. As a family we prayed earnestly that each one of them would consider the message of love from God and respond positively by receiving Christ personally.

Arriving home before dark, I felt a need to go to the hospital to see my mother. I entered her hospital room and immediately sensed her apprehensive spirit. She asked about every detail of the trip as well as the worship service and appeared to be genuinely delighted to hear that both my sisters and my two cousins had enjoyed the day.

Finally, with the small talk out of the way, she began to share the events of her day.

"Carole, today I had two very special visitors," she told me, her eyes filling with tears.

"Who came to see you?" I inquired.

"Do you remember my telling you that I was married and divorced long ago?"

"Of course," I said. How could I forget after Grandmother Clark's conversation with me years ago? I thought it strange that she would want to talk about her first marriage after thirty-two years of silence, and I wondered how her two mysterious visitors could be connected to such a forgotten past.

Then, like a small child cautiously seeking approval, Mama began to tell me the events leading up to her unusual day. For the past forty-eight years Mama had had no contact with her former husband. He and his wife lived in the same general area, however, and they maintained a friendship with Mama's aunt and uncle. Now I understood why Mama had always insisted on calling her aunt before our family visited. She must have feared an accidental meeting between us and her former husband and his wife, an uncomfortable situation for both parties.

Continuing with her story, Mama told me that her aunt had recently delivered a very disturbing message. It seemed Mama's former husband had asked her to convey a message. He wanted to ask Mama to forgive him for all the hurt he had caused in her life. This was beginning to sound like a romance novel instead of real life.

Mama said that she was angry that he would even want to contact her, but after giving it more thought, she decided she would agree to see him after all these years. At least it would satisfy her curiosity. The opportunity came while all three of her daughters were traveling out of town on the same day.

At her request Daddy placed a phone call to this man and suggested he come to the hospital for a visit, stressing that he also bring his wife. If there was going to be a conversation about forgiveness after forty-eight years, Mama wanted both her former husband and his wife to be involved. Daddy did not want to be present. He had no objection to her plans, but neither had he any interest in participating in such an unusual meeting.

Mama had been so insistent that my two sisters choose that particular Sunday to go to Atlanta with me; now I understood her reasoning. The timing was perfect. It made it easier, having us all out of town. She did not want us to even know about this meeting much less be involved in it in any way.

I listened intently as she described the meeting that had taken place that afternoon. Daddy had left to go home about 2:30 in the afternoon. Once she was alone, she walked out to the main lobby of the hospital and found a seat in the corner of the waiting room. From this unnoticed spot, she watched, hoping to catch a glimpse of her expected visitors. Like a child trying to justify her action, she explained that she had just wanted to know what to expect. Tears flowed unashamedly down her face.

"Carole, when I saw them, my heart was saddened," she said. "Although his body is crippled with severe arthritis, he and his wife walked hand in hand, as if they were unaware of the passage of years. She showed such tenderness toward him. I believe they are very much in love, even after forty-eight years."

By this time I was crying. The tenderness of the moment was so different from Mama's normal hostility. She had been known as "hardhearted Hannah" for as long as I could remember, yet here she was, talking of two people she had hated and weeping for their love and caring. I knew something very special had occurred that day.

"Slipping out of the lobby, I made my way back to my room and anxiously waited for their arrival," she told me. "Would you believe that no other visitors came while they were here? It was as if that time was for our reunion, without interruption."

"What happened when they came in?" I asked, wanting to hear every detail.

"It was very special," she said, as if still amazed herself. "After a little small talk about our health difficulties, he simply thanked me for agreeing to see him. Then he told me how grateful he was that I had included his wife."

"Carole, they both asked me to forgive them," she said almost in disbelief. "I thought for a moment and wondered how I could just wipe out all the hurt and pain they had caused in my life. I was not sure I even wanted to give them the pleasure of forgiveness."

With an openness to reason that was new to Mama, she began to explain her thoughts and feelings as I had never heard her do before.

"A strange thing happened," she said almost apologetically. "I remembered that when we pray the Lord's Prayer, we ask God to forgive us—as we forgive others. Suddenly, I knew that I had never forgiven them and therefore had no right to ask God to forgive me."

"So I forgave them!" she said boldly. "It felt so good to give forgiveness and to be able to ask for it in return. There were no strings attached."

This day had been more than I could have expected. My heart was overflowing with joy, and Mama and I hugged and wept openly. I had come prepared to spend the night, but Mama refused. She insisted that she no longer needed anyone at night. It had been a busy day for her and she felt she would sleep well, knowing things were better in her heart. After arriving safely at home, I shared excitedly with Jimmy all that had happened. It was a memorable day.

That week brought more unexpected joy. The doctor dismissed Mama from the hospital, and she seemed anxious to go home. The evening of her first day home, Jimmy and I went over to visit. When we arrived, Daddy told me that Mama wanted to see me, *alone*. Nothing was said between Daddy and me about Mama's visitors, and I don't know if he even knew that I had been told. So Jimmy visited with Daddy, and I went in to see Mama.

I entered the dimly lit bedroom. I felt Mama had a purpose in our private meeting. It seemed strange that she wanted to remain in the shadows, but she motioned for me to sit in the chair next to her bed and wasted no time in taking charge of the conversation.

"Carole," she said, as if checking off a list of things to discuss, "I want to go to church in Atlanta with you and Jimmy as soon as I am able."

I was shocked. Could this be my mother? Up to this time she had ridiculed our trips to attend a church that was different from the one we had grown up in. Her resentment seemed to have given way to a genuine interest. When I asked why she had decided to visit, she replied without any hesitation.

"I have never seen anything have such a profound effect on your sister. All she talks about is this church," she said. "Now I want to go and see what makes it different."

Seizing the opportunity before she changed her mind, I quickly expressed my delight.

"Mama," I said, "in a couple of weeks the sanctuary choir and orchestra will be presenting an afternoon musical program. I think that would be a perfect time for you to go."

She seemed pleased that I had agreed so quickly and that I had not questioned her reasons. I knew that music played a significant part in Mama's life, and the timing of this concert was perfect. If anything could speak to Mama, it would probably be music. It was well known in our family that music was Mama's therapy. Often, in the dark, she would sit at her piano and play one song after the other. We also knew that when Mama whistled while she washed dishes or cooked a meal, she was upset about something. Best leave her alone until she whistled it out of her system.

"Carole, I need to tell you something about me that you don't know," she offered.

My world around was changing so drastically. One more surprise seemed somewhat in order. I listened as she related her experiences that began some forty-eight years earlier. Memories previously locked up tight inside her heart began to pour out like a rushing stream. She talked about her mental breakdown, the horrible hospitalization in the state mental hospital and her slow recovery. For the first time she shared the intense pain and heartbreak of having her young husband, whom she loved dearly, reject her for the nurse he had hired to take care of her. Then, as if the pain was still fresh, she relived the emptiness of feeling so betrayed and isolated. Afraid to let any one know of her past, she had carefully and unknowingly built a foreboding wall of defense.

She talked about the frustration she experienced through the years, hearing of others who suffered with mental illness and fearing her own dark secret might be revealed. She told me that from the beginning of her recovery, she had heeded the specific advice of her family physician and her pastor to guard her past from those who did not already know. They told her that anyone she told, especially her children, would reject her and not love her. The unfounded belief that any knowledge of her past would bring further rejection and ridicule from those she loved kept her imprisoned in her own private pain.

In that dark room she wept uncontrollably. She told me about how my older sister's own mental illness had frightened her and made her worry about heredity and environment. Unknown to us, she had struggled with intense shame and even felt somehow responsible for my sister's illness.

For more than an hour I listened and felt her pain. By now I was crying also, but for a different reason. There was no blame or rejection on my part. I was angry that false information and undeserved shame had robbed her of the freedom she could have experienced for so many years. My love for her was deeper than ever, and I was grateful to have had this time of special bonding.

It was clear to me why she preferred the dimly lit room. There was a measure of comfort and safety in the shadows. She still feared rejection, but my quietness and acceptance had paved the way for Mama to open up to me.

"Mama," I said, "thank you for sharing these painful memories with me, but I knew most of this already."

"You knew! How did you know?" she asked tearfully.

Now I was glad for the shadows in the room. I didn't want to hurt Mama, and I certainly didn't want to reveal my source. But we had come this far, and nothing was going to stop the honesty that was needed.

"Several years ago," I began, "when I was struggling to understand why you were so hostile, I asked Jimmy's grandmother if she could help me make sense out of your apparent anger. Being the wise and compassionate woman that she was, Grandmother Clark told me all of the story that she knew. She told me about your illness, your hospitalization, and your divorce. I wanted to tell you that I knew, but she told me I couldn't."

There was a brief moment of silence. If I live to be a hundred I will never forget Mama's next words.

"You knew? And you still loved me?"

"Oh yes, Mama. I have always loved you. Now I love you even more!"

As we hugged, we experienced the joy of unconditional love between a mother and daughter for the very first time, and I knew nothing could ever separate us again. Before I left the room we agreed to plan the trip to Atlanta in two weeks. Somehow I felt confident that it would be a special time of celebration for our new relationship.

Daddy expressed no desire to go with us to Atlanta, but my younger sister seemed anxious to be a part of this special day. We drove two cars and left home about six in the morning. After a three-hour trip, we arrived at the church. Jimmy and I were so excited we could hardly contain our joy. Mama was both impressed with the musical choruses we sang as a congregation and was spellbound with the morning message.

After lunch we hurried back to the church for the concert at three o'clock. The choir was presenting a musical, *A Praise Gathering for Believers* by Bill Gaither. We were not disappointed. Mama was thrilled with the beautiful music and did not seem to be tired from such a busy day. The trip home was easy. Our prayers had been answered. Sometime the next day I called Mama on the phone, and it was such a delight to hear her talk so positively about the church that our family had grown to love.

"All morning I have been singing one song that I heard yesterday, but I can't remember all of the words," she said.

"Sing the song and maybe I can fill in the words," I replied.

With no further prompting she began singing, "*Something beautiful, something good! All my confusion, He understood. All I had to offer Him was...and...; and He made something beautiful of my life.* What are the two words that I can't remember?" she asked.

My heart raced with excitement. This was not only about the two missing words of a song, but the true answer to Mama's life. Trembling at the prospect of once again being able to share the simple message of salvation with my precious mother, I blurted out, *brokenness and strife*, Mama; that is all any of us has to offer! He can make something beautiful of your life!"

"That's it," she said with a sigh of relief. "I can do that."

And she did! Mama knew what it meant to be forgiven and free. Her past was no longer a threat to her peace of mind. She was loved and accepted by God. Just like my great-aunt had transformed my moth-eaten sweater into a one-of-a-kind designer original, God had taken Mama's brokenness and strife and began the process that was to amaze family and friends alike. Mama became a one-of-a-kind original creation.

Let's Consider the Lion of Rejection

Rejection, either real or imagined, can be a crippling emotion. It is real when isolation results. For instance, when there is a clear disagreement regarding someone's beliefs, actions, or lifestyle, we allow rejection by denying fellowship.

Likewise, when we project our feelings or attitudes on someone else without any explanation, rejection becomes imagined. A false assumption can be the tool to construct a wall of alienation. For example, rather than risk exposure of her past, my mother found security in imagined rejection. The very people who would have been willing to reach out to her in love were kept at arm's length for forty-eight years.

Life has taught me that it is not for our weaknesses that we suffer rejection so much as it is for our strengths. Mama did not reject me because I was weak but because of the unexplainable strength she could see. It was a threat to her own security. In a self-protective mindset, it seems more advantageous to push away what we do not understand than to openly embrace something new.

The opposite of rejection is acceptance. This begins with, first of all, acceptance of who and where we are. If we feel inferior to others, ashamed of our circumstances or fearful of exposure, we will miss out on God's best plan for our lives.

To build relationships and experience growth, we must be willing to accept those who are different. It would certainly be boring if all of us were exactly the same. The chosen motto of Christian Women's Clubs is: In essentials unity, in nonessentials charity, and in all things to glorify Christ. That is a very healthy foundation stone to build upon.

Once again the choice is mine and yours. Life is full of brokenness and strife. Sometimes it comes from circumstances beyond our control, while at other times it is by our own design. You must make a life-changing decision to either accept and go on or allow defeat to rob you of your productivity. You cannot remain neutral. How are you coping with the rejection in your life?

Romans 8:28 reminds us that God is at work in "all things"— not just in isolated events. God never promised us that we would have a life free from difficulty or that every detail of life would be fair according to what men count as fairness. We live in a fallen world where evil is prevalent. But He is able to turn every frustration and rejection into a powerful tool to bring ultimate good into our lives.

Why is it that some people live in bondage to rejection— either real or imagined—when there is a way out? It can be a simple matter of choice. The promise found in Romans 8:28 is for those who love God and answer the call to live according to His purpose. God's purpose is to make us like Christ.

As our role model, Christ suffered rejection from His own family, but it did not hinder His life's work. He could have complained about the less than comfortable circumstances of life, but He knew His Heavenly Father was in control. Acceptance was evident in His life, even as He went to Calvary. But remember, without the cruel cross there would be no need for the empty tomb. Out of the darkness came the resurrection.

What about your life? Do you struggle with rejection because of disappointments and preconceived ideas? Do you believe God can make something beautiful from the brokenness and strife you know best? Are you willing to trust God to give you a new perspective on your circumstances? Are you willing to release your bitterness? Can you genuinely forgive those who may have caused you emotional pain?

Then why not, in an act of surrender, release the circumstances that have brought rejection and allow God to "work all things" out according to His will. He can make *something beautiful* of your life, if you let Him.

We have not arrived. What I mean is we have not completed our journey and fulfilled God's purpose for our life. You and I still live in a world dominated with pain, injustice, and suffering. Although we are looking for the day when we will reside in heaven with our Lord and Savior Jesus Christ, we are not home yet.

Paul the Apostle could say, "Forget what is behind, stretch forth to what is ahead and keep pressing on toward the intended goal for your life—to know Jesus Christ and enjoy Him forever" (Philippians 3:14).

Let's press on together!

EPILOGUE

୧୬୦୨

Dear Friend,

It is my desire above all else in this "journey" we have just traveled together that you have caught a fresh glimpse of freedom—for whom the Son sets free is free indeed!

Perhaps you have identified similar lions in your own life or have gained knowledge and understanding of the struggles that others face day in and day out.

Life is a journey—there are detours to maneuver, mountains to climb, deserts to cross, and potholes to avoid. But the best part of any journey is learning to enjoy the trip until you arrive at the intended destination. Although my life has sometimes been difficult, it is the constant presence of the mighty, living, Son of God—Jesus Christ—that makes my feet as surefooted as a deer and takes me to high places never seen before. I am not afraid, for He walks with me and He tells me I am his own. I am encouraged by the fact that He cares so deeply for me, just an ordinary person. As it says in Romans 8:31: "If God be for us, who can be against us?"

Every time I stand before an audience of strangers, I am overwhelmed with the faithfulness of God. Remembering that day in January of 1970 when God spoke to my heart about trusting Him for the journey, I know He has done something very special in my life. The joy I have in sharing my experiences and the lessons I've learned is multiplied time and time again when those who have been dealing with lions, both real and imagined, experience victory through Christ.

Some of my experiences have been painful to recall, while others have been embarrassing. If they have filled your heart with pain or possibly have struck a familiar chord of despair, please know that my prayer has been for you to somehow grow closer to Him.

My life since experiencing the "new birth" in September 1969 has been an open book. No more games, no hiding behind masks, and no pretending. Believing that God wants me to be as transparent as clear glass, I have willingly shared details with you to let you see the glory of God in the life of a sinner saved by grace!

Along our journey you have been introduced to my family through various circumstances, and I would like to bring you up to date.

Jimmy and I are celebrating forty-plus years of marriage, a deepening friendship, and a growing oneness in Jesus Christ. We strive to practice, in all of our relationships, the victory of unconditional love. We are cofounders of Higher Ground, Inc., a ministry designed to help travelers of all ages press on to the prize of the high calling of God in Christ Jesus. We are interdenominational and maintain a strong evangelistic message that reaches those who have a desire to be all they were created to be in Jesus.

Our journey has not been without twists and turns, however. We faced our greatest lion in December 1991 when Jimmy was diagnosed with a high-grade malignant cancer in the salivary glands of his face. The cancer was aggressive and so was the treatment. After eight surgeries in one year, thirty-three radiation treatments, and six months of chemotherapy, Jimmy has survived. Then in December of 1996 came prostate cancer and recently a melanoma on his back, both detected in the early stages. Today he is feeling fine, praising God for each day, and able to live life at its best.

God is so good to us. Through all his treatments, Jimmy never wavered in his faith, continued to share the overcoming power of God in his life, and adjusted to his new limitations with grace. He is a very good patient and continues to surprise all who meet him with his positive attitude.

"After all," he says, "I know God loves me and has a plan for my life, so why worry?"

His ministry of sharing continues on a one-on-one basis or as a guest speaker for church and civic groups, as well as at Christian Women's and Couple's Clubs.

My father, Joe Hammond, died of cancer on June 24, 1976. I am sad to say that I did not witness any real evidence of Jesus in his heart and life.

Just fourteen months later, my mother, Eleanor P. Hammond, died on September 4, 1977, of a heart attack. I feel with all my heart that she finished her earthly journey and is now in a place where there is no fear of rejection.

Jimmy's mother, Opal H. Bequest, suffered a massive stoke in September of 1987 and was unable to speak or take care of herself for almost six years. She died in June of 1993 a very sad and lonely lady.

Jamey, our oldest son, is married to Cheryl, and they have four daughters—Priscilla, Liorah, Ramona, and Moriah. They live in Franklin, Virginia.

Jody, our second son, is married to Roxanne, and they have one daughter—Audrey. They live in Martinez, Georgia.

Lael, our third son, is married to Lynne, and they have one daughter—Sophia. They live in Cumming, Georgia.

Leda, our only daughter, is married to Ian Goodman, and they have one son—Christopher. They live in Chattanooga, Tennessee.

I speak approximately forty times a year at Christian Women's Clubs. Through our Higher Ground ministry, I have the privilege of leading five Bible studies, speaking for mother-daughter banquets, and leading retreats. God has given me a fruitful one-on-one ministry of reconciliation. Of course, my schedule is always arranged to provide priceless family time with our children and grandchildren.

Remember, I only had one goal for life—I wanted to meet a good-looking Christian man, get married, have four to six children, and live happily ever after. Well, through God's plan for my life, not my own devices, I married that good-looking man—Jimmy Camak. He is even more handsome today—his blue eyes sparkle with the love of Christ, and his gray hair frames a face that, though scarred by cancer, reflects the transforming work of the Holy Spirit. We had six children and had the joy of raising four. Best of all, we all will live happily ever after, because along with us, our children have received the One who died for them—Jesus Christ, the mighty Son of God. We have no greater joy than to know that our children walk in truth.

Thank you for spending some of your time walking through the journey with me. May God bless you, and remember this: *Jesus sets you free to be all you were meant to be!*

To order additional copies of

There Came a Lion

send $10.95 + $3.95 shipping and handling to:

Carole H. Camak
P.O. Box 457
Grovetown, GA
30813